...t established
...ravel brands,
...erts in travel.

...35 years our
...d the secrets
...d the world,
...a wealth of
...perience and a passion for travel.

**Rely on Thomas Cook as your
travelling companion on your next trip
and benefit from our unique heritage.**

Thomas Cook **pocket** guides

SKIATHOS
SKOPELOS & ALONNISOS

Thos Cook

Your travelling companion since 1873

Updated by Chris Deliso

Published by Thomas Cook Publishing
A division of Thomas Cook Tour Operations Limited
Company registration no. 3772199 England
The Thomas Cook Business Park, Unit 9, Coningsby Road,
Peterborough PE3 8SB, United Kingdom
Email: books@thomascook.com, Tel: +44 (0) 1733 416477
www.thomascookpublishing.com

Produced by Cambridge Publishing Management Limited
Burr Elm Court, Main Street, Caldecote CB23 7NU
www.cambridgepm.co.uk

ISBN: 978-1-84848-387-3

First edition © 2009 Thomas Cook Publishing
This second edition © 2011 Thomas Cook Publishing
Text © Thomas Cook Publishing
Maps © Thomas Cook Publishing/PCGraphics (UK) Limited

Series Editor: Karen Beaulah
Production/DTP: Steven Collins

Printed and bound in Spain by GraphyCems

Cover photography © Thomas Cook Publishing

CONTENTS

WHAT'S IN YOUR GUIDEBOOK?

Independent authors Impartial, up-to-date information from our travel experts who meticulously source local knowledge.

Experience Thomas Cook's 165 years in the travel industry and guidebook publishing enriches every word with expertise you can trust.

Travel know-how Thomas Cook has thousands of staff working around the globe, all living and breathing travel.

Editors Travel-publishing professionals, pulling everything together to craft a perfect blend of words, pictures, maps and design.

You, the traveller We deliver a practical, no-nonsense approach to information, geared to how you really use it.

Clear water and white sand at Ambelakia beach, Skiathos

 # INTRODUCTION
Getting to know Skiathos, Skopelos & Alonnisos

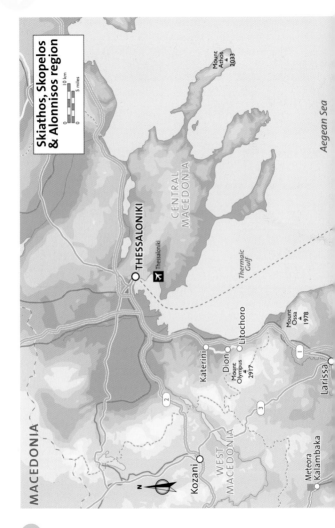

Skiathos, Skopelos
& Alonnisos region

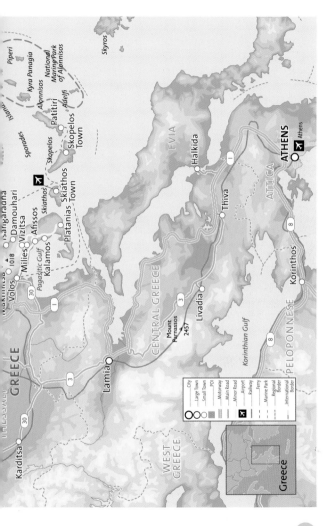

Piperi

Skyros

Kyra Panagia

National Marine Park of Alonnisos

Alonnisos

Pattiri

Adelfi

Skopelos

Skopelos Town

Sporades

EVIA

ATHENS

Athens

Halkida

Skiathos

Skiathos Town

Platanias

ATTICA

Sangaradna

Damouhari

Vizitsa

Afissos

Kalamos

Pagasitic Gulf

Milies

1018

Volos

Thiva

Korinthos

30

1

CENTRAL GREECE

Livadia

3

Korinthian Gulf

8

Mount Parnassos

2457

GREECE

3

Lamia

1

PELOPONNESE

30

Karditsa

City

Large Town

Small Town

POI

Motorway

Main Road

Minor Road

Airport

Railway

Ferry

Marine Park

Regional Border

International Border

WEST GREECE

Greece

Getting to know Skiathos, Skopelos & Alonnisos

Skiathos, Skopelos and Alonnisos are the main holiday islands of the Sporades, the Greek archipelago some 120 km (74½ miles) long and 40 km (25 miles) wide that is scattered in the Aegean Sea. The Sporades stretch southeastwards from the tip of the Pilion peninsula, midway up the eastern coast of mainland Greece. Skiathos, Skopelos and Alonnisos lie within sight of each other, while lonely Skyros, the largest but least visited of the four, is set apart from the others, around 60 km (37 miles) southeast of its sisters. Northeast of Alonnisos, a scattering of much smaller, uninhabited islets lie within the boundaries of the National Marine Park of Alonnisos.

Skiathos is probably the best known of these islands, and almost everyone who comes to Skiathos has been drawn by the allure of its beaches, which include some of the best sandy strands in the Aegean and have been awarded a plethora of Blue Flags. Skopelos and Alonnisos are less well endowed with fine golden sand, but have plenty of blue-water bays lined with white pebbles and shingle. The wonderful beaches, along with pretty villages, pine-covered hills and a perfect climate, make the Sporades one of the most favoured holiday destinations in the Aegean, with each of the islands offering distinctively different delights.

Getting to the Sporades is easily done with a direct flight to Skiathos. Skiathos' airport – which handles charter flights from major British and

SKYROS & EVIA

The island of Skyros, far to the east of Skiathos, is also (technically) part of the Sporades island group, as is the much larger island of Evia, which hugs the mainland to the south. There are one or two daily ferries in summer from Evia to Skyros (€9) and two weekly ferries in summer from Skyros to Alonnisos and then Skopelos (€22).

European cities in summer, as well as domestic flights from Greece's big cities – is only 3 km (2 miles) from the town centre. To get to the other islands, fast hydrofoils and ferries leave frequently from Skiathos Town's bustling waterfront, connecting Skiathos with its near neighbours, Skopelos and Alonnisos, and with the mainland port of Volos.

⬤ *The red roofs and bustling harbour of Skiathos Town*

THE BEST OF SKIATHOS, SKOPELOS & ALONNISOS

TOP 10 ATTRACTIONS

- **Golden sands** Some say Koukounaries, on the south coast of Skiathos, is the best beach in Greece; in fact, it's a string of three soft, sandy (and far from uncrowded) beaches, with plenty of summer cantinas and watersports (see pages 26–33).

- **Make the party scene** Vromolimnos, midway between Koukounaries and Skiathos Town, is the liveliest party beach in the Sporades, with watersports, bungee jumping and loud music bars (see page 36).

- **Ghost village** Visit the spooky, deserted hilltop village of Kastro, where the islanders of Skiathos took refuge from Turkish raiders in the 14th century (see pages 18 & 20).

- **Seals and dolphins** Take a boat trip to the deserted islands of the National Marine Park of Alonnisos, home to endangered monk seals, dolphins, turtles and rare seabirds (see pages 51 & 61–2).

- **Beneath the waves** Dive the clear blue waters at spots such as Tsougria, the desert island only five minutes from Skiathos, and meet moray eels, grouper and octopus (see pages 20 & 22).

- **Saddle up** and go horse or donkey riding along old mule trails in the wooded hills of Skiathos (see page 30).

- **Cliff-top monasteries** Drive to the awesome medieval monasteries of the Meteora, perched atop towering basalt pinnacles above the plains of Thessaly (see pages 75–6).

- **Home of the gods** Visit Mount Olympus, Greece's highest mountain, and the ruins of ancient Dion on its lower slopes (see pages 83–5).

- **Acropolis now** Athens, Greece's capital, with its ancient heritage, super shopping and mesmerising museums, makes an excellent excursion by air or by road (see pages 69–73).

- **City adventure** Greece's second city, Thessaloniki, can be visited from Skiathos by fast hydrofoil and is crammed with fascinating history and excellent restaurants (see pages 86–92).

◆ *The popular golden sand beach at Agia Paraskevi, Skiathos*

SYMBOLS KEY
The following symbols are used throughout this book:

ⓐ address 📞 telephone ⓦ website address ⓔ email
🕐 opening times Ⓝ public transport ❶ important

The following symbols are used on the maps:

𝒊 information office	○ city
✉ post office	○ large town
🛍 shopping	○ small town
✈ airport	◼ point of interest
✚ hospital	══ motorway
🕑 police station	━ main road
🚌 bus station	─ minor road
🚆 railway station	─ railway
✝ church	Ⓜ metro
❶ numbers denote featured cafés, restaurants & evening venues		

RESTAURANT CATEGORIES
The symbol after the name of each restaurant listed in this guide
indicates the price of a typical three-course meal without drinks
for one person.
£ under €20   ££ €20–€35   £££ over €35

▶ *Big Banana beach, in the south of Skiathos*

RESORTS
Places under the sun

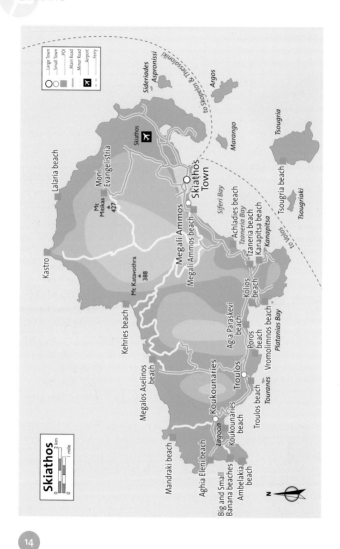

Skiathos

0 ——— 2 km
0 ——— 1 mile

- ○ Large Town
- ● Small Town
- POI
- Main Road
- Minor Road
- ✈ Airport
- Ferry

to Skopelos & Thessaloniki

Sideriades
Aspronissi
Argos
Marango
Tsougria
Tsougria beach
Tsougriaki

Skiathos ✈
Skiathos Town

Moni Evangelistria
Lalaria beach

Mt Mtiokas
427

Siferi Bay
Achladies beach
Tzaneria Bay
Tzaneria beach
Kanapitsa beach
Kanapitsa

Megali Ammos
Megali Ammos beach

to Volos

Kastro

Mt Katavothra
388

Kolios beach

Kehries beach

Agia Paraskevi beach
Poros beach
Vromolimnos beach
Platanias Bay

Megalos Aselinos beach

Koukounaries
Troulos
Touranes
Troulos beach

Mandraki beach

Lagoon
Koukounaries beach

Aghia Eleni beach

Big and Small Banana beaches
Ambelakia beach

N

Skiathos Town

Postcard-pretty Skiathos Town, the island's 'capital', is the only large town on the island. It is built on two low hills, rising above twin harbours – the Old Port and the New Port – where smart sailing yachts, luxurious motor cruisers and excursion boats now outnumber the dwindling fleet of fishing boats.

Just offshore, and connected to the harbour esplanade by a short causeway, the tiny, pine-covered Bourtzi island juts into the bay, separating Skiathos' old fishing harbour from the new yacht and ferry harbour. Once the site of a medieval Venetian fortress (of which nothing remains except some dilapidated foundations), Bourtzi is now home to the island's theatre and a pleasant open-air café under the pine trees, with great views across the vividly blue water to the little uninhabited islands of Tsougria and Tsougriaki and – on a clear day – to Evia, the second-largest island in Greece after Crete.

The town's narrow streets are lined with whitewashed houses, typically with bright-painted wrought-iron balconies, red-tiled roofs, wooden shutters and small courtyards made more colourful by pots of geraniums and basil, and clumps of purple and scarlet bougainvillea.

There are beaches within walking distance, and Skiathos Town is well endowed with pubs, bars and cafés beside its two pretty harbours. There are plenty of restaurants, and the harbour esplanade is also lined with car- and bike-rental outfits and travel and tour agencies. Day-trip boats and water-taxis leave every morning for the busy beaches along the south coast of the island, and for the less crowded strands on the north and east coasts.

Skiathos Town has a lively enough nightlife scene, with a handful of open-air discos and a row of laid-back clubs and music bars east of the yacht marina, about five minutes' walk from the centre. However, even in high season, there is none of the rowdiness that mars some of the noisier Greek islands.

To many visitors, Skiathos Town looks surprisingly Italian, with the campaniles (bell towers) of three pretty churches rising above the

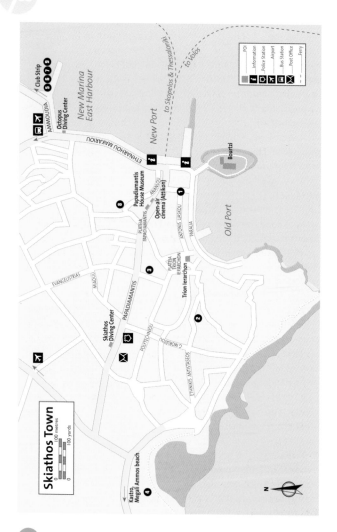

Skiathos Town

0 100 metres
0 100 yards

N

to Skopelos & Thessaloníki
to Vólos

New Marina
East Harbour

Club Strip ❽❼❾

AMMOUDIA
Octopus Diving Center

ETHNARHOU MAKARIOU

New Port

Bourtzi

Old Port

Papadiamantis House Museum ❽

Open-air cinema (Attikon)

MITROPOLEOS
PLATEIA PAPADIAMANTIS

❶

ANTONIS IASSOU
PARALIA

❸

Trion Ierarchon

PLATEIA TRION IERARCHON

EVANGELISTRIAS

MIAOULI

PAPADIAMANTIS

Skiathos Diving Center

POLYTECHNIOU

G MOURTZOU

❷

ETHNIKIS ANTISTASOS

Kastro, Megáli Ammos beach

❹

POI
Information
Police Station
Airport
Bus Station
Post Office
Ferry

red-tiled roofs of 18th-century houses. Compared with many Greek settlements, it's quite a modern town. For many centuries, the island was frequently pillaged by Turkish corsairs and most islanders lived in the fortified village of Kastro, high above the sea on the north tip of Skiathos. In the 1830s, when the Sporades, along with most of Greece, gained independence from the Ottoman Empire, the islanders abandoned Kastro and built Skiathos Town, beside a fine natural harbour. Skiathos also attracted the attention of the Franks and the Venetians, who vied with the Turks and the Byzantine Empire for control of the Aegean islands for more than 400 years and built a small fortress on Bourtzi island.

BEACHES

Skiathos boasts over 60 beaches; the fine beaches of Skiathos' south coast are easily accessible from Skiathos Town, with buses leaving the town centre every 15 minutes during the day and stopping at all the most popular resorts. The town also has its own beaches within walking distance of the harbour.

Bourtzi

Bourtzi is not so much a beach, more a bathing spot below the terrace of the Bourtzi café-bar, with a springboard and ladder giving access to the clean, clear water around this little pine-covered peninsula. Perhaps not perfect for an entire day, but conveniently located for a pre-lunch dip when you're visiting Skiathos Town. There are changing cubicles and immaculately clean toilets next to the café. There's also a tiny sand and pebble beach on the west side of the causeway that links Bourtzi to the waterfront, where children can paddle and swim.

Megali Ammos

On any other Greek island, Megali Ammos would qualify as one of the top beaches. On Skiathos, it is admittedly outshone by the even finer beaches further west. It has the advantage of being within walking distance of town (the east end of Megali Ammos is only five minutes' walk from the harbour), the beach is lined with lively bars and restaurants, the sand is clean and the water is crystalline. The east end of the beach, which has the best sand, is predictably the busiest – it's a favourite with locals – but Megali Ammos becomes less crowded as you walk west, with long stretches of gravelly sand mixed with small pebbles. There are lifeguards and changing rooms near the west end of the beach, where watersports are also available.

THINGS TO SEE & DO

Attikon (open-air cinema)
Skiathos Town's open-air cinema, shows the latest releases twice nightly, with two different films each week, and has its own snack bar. All films are in English with Greek subtitles. ⓐ Papadiamantis (signposted, opposite the National Bank of Greece) ☎ 24270 22352
🕒 Bar opens 20.30, first showing 21.00 ❶ Admission charge

Island cruises
Four excursion boats operated by the local boat-owners' cooperative sail from the 'Old Port' on round-the-island cruises taking in sea-caves, the north-coast beaches at Lalaria and Megalos Aselinos (where you stop for lunch) and Tsougria island. Tickets are sold on board. Water-taxis also leave hourly from the Old Port for the beaches at Kanapitsa and Achladies.
Excursion boats ⓐ Old Port 🕒 Depart 10.00, return 17.00

WHAT'S IN A NAME?
Skiathos can be translated as 'the shadow of Athos' and although Mount Athos, Greece's famous 'Holy Mountain' (far to the northeast of Skiathos), is usually hidden by summer haze, it can be seen on clear spring and autumn days and on mornings after a summer rain storm. The Athos peninsula is inhabited only by Greek Orthodox monks, who dwell in around 30 picturesque medieval monasteries.

⬤ *Skiathos Town is built on low hills*

Kastro and the monasteries

The deserted, formerly fortified hilltop village that was home to most of the island's inhabitants from the 14th century until the 1830s is about 16 km (10 miles) north of Skiathos Town and is accessed by very rough roads that really require a 4WD vehicle. In its heyday, it was home to several thousand people and had around 30 Orthodox churches and chapels. Most of these have vanished, but Christos sto Kastro (the Church of Christ) – a sturdy 17th-century basilica with some fine mural paintings – survives and is well worth a look.

A trip to Kastro can be combined with a visit to one or more of the island's historic monasteries, on the slopes of Mount Mitikas, between Skiathos Town and Kastro. The most important of these is **Moni Evangelistria** (🕐 09.30–13.30, 17.00–19.00 daily), an imposing building of grey local stone that stands just below Karaflytzanaka, the highest peak on the island. There's a museum and shop at the monastery, too.

Papadiamantis House Museum

This pretty little museum is tucked away on a small square just off Skiathos Town's main shopping street. It celebrates the life of the island's most famous son, the journalist, philosopher and author, Alexandros Papadiamantis (1851–1911). The house, where the writer died in 1911, with its plain wooden floors, tiny bedrooms and simple furniture, is a typical old-fashioned island home and is adorned with photos, manuscripts and portraits of the author. 🄰 Plateia Papadiamantis ☎ 24270 23843 🕐 09.30–13.30, 17.00–20.30 Tues–Sun

Scuba diving

With normally calm seas and excellent underwater visibility, Skiathos is a good place to learn to dive or take a refresher course. There is plenty to see, with an array of undersea life from octopus and lobster to colourful reef creatures and bigger fish such as grouper. It also offers some more challenging dive sites for experienced and advanced divers. Night dives, snorkelling trips and 'free diving' (deep diving without scuba equipment) are also on offer.

⬤ *The attractive bell and clock tower above Skiathos Town*

Octopus Diving Center ⓐ East Harbour, Ethnarhou Makariou ❶ 24270 24549, 69441 68958 (mobile) Ⓦ www.odc-skiathos.com ⓛ Information and bookings on board in harbour 19.30–23.30

Skiathos Diving Center ⓐ Papadiamantis, Akropolis ❶ 24270 24424 Ⓦ www.skiathosdivingcenter.gr

Trion Ierarchon

The elegant bell tower of this Italianate church is an unmissable landmark in the town centre, overlooking the old harbour. Built in 1846, it is famed for the supposedly miracle-working icon of Panaghia Eikonistria, which was discovered here in 1650. ⓐ Plateia Trion Ierarchon ⓛ Dawn until dusk

Watersports

Waterskiing, parascending and kayaking are among the thrills on offer at the east end of Megali Ammos beach. **Megali Ammos Watersports** ⓐ Megali Ammos beach ❶ 24270 23492 ⓛ 10.00–18.00 daily

Yacht sailing

Crewed yachts sail on day trips from the New Marina at the east side of the New Port, taking you to the pretty uninhabited island of Tsougria, neighbouring Skopelos, or further afield. Most day cruises include a picnic or lunch in a seaside taverna, pauses for swimming and sunbathing, drinks and snacks.

Argo III has an entertaining skipper and provides home-cooked lunches and drinks at any time. ⓐ New Marina, Ethnarhou Makariou ❶ 69323 25167 (mobile) ⓛ Depart 10.30, return 17.00

Voula of London is a smaller boat that does not provide food. ⓐ New Marina, Ethnarhou Makariou ❶ 69788 30401 (mobile) ⓛ Depart 10.15, return 18.00, bookings taken on board 19.00–22.30

TAKING A BREAK

Koziakas £ ❶ Traditional grill restaurant on the street that runs parallel to the Old Port waterfront, with a meat-heavy menu, chicken, pork and lamb and Greek favourites such as *kokoretsi*. ❷ Antonis Liaskou, Old Port ❶ 24270 23297 ⏱ 12.00–16.00, 19.00–24.00 daily

Ta Bakaliarakia ££ ❷ This venerable restaurant, founded in 1958, claims to be the oldest eating place on Skiathos and offers excellent traditional cooking with a menu that ranges from rabbit stew and cod croquettes to a big choice of salads and 'bites for wine' such as 'fried entrails' and 'boiled paw of beef'. ❷ Corner of Epifaniou Dimitriou and Grigoriou 5 ❶ 24270 22588 ⏱ 12.00–15.00, 20.00–23.00 daily

Bonaparte Restaurant ££ ❸ This slightly upmarket place serves inventive international cuisine with an Asian flourish. It's located on a quiet side street off Papadiamantis. ❷ Odos Evangelistrias ❶ 24270 21118 ⏱ 09.00–24.00 daily

Taverna Twilight ££ ❹ Good traditional Greek cooking within walking distance of the centre, at the east end of the beach. ❷ Bus stop 6, Megali Ammos beach ❶ 24270 23050 ⏱ 12.00–23.00 daily

Carnayo £££ ❺ Carnayo has enjoyed a reputation as a great place to eat on Skiathos since it opened in 1975. Its varied menu has a strongly Italian flavour (lots of steaks in imaginative sauces, pasta and seafood). ❷ Nea Paralia (east end of Ethnarhou Makariou) ❶ 24270 22868 Ⓦ www.carnayo.gr ⏱ 12.00–15.00, 20.00–24.00 daily

Scuna £££ ❻ With an attractive location overlooking the yacht marina, and a menu that combines Greek and Mediterranean influences, this is probably the best restaurant in Skiathos Town. ❷ Nea Paralia, Ammoudia ❶ 24270 22185 ⏱ 12.00–15.00, 19.00–23.00 daily

AFTER DARK

Polytechniou, which runs parallel to Papadiamantis, is the town's bar street, with more than a dozen places to hang out after sundown.

⬤ *A memorial to Skiathos' sailors on the waterfront*

Skiathos Town's 'Club Strip' is east of the town centre and the marina, along the stretch of shoreline called Ammoudia.

LIVE MUSIC

Milos Taverna £ ❼ Tables stand by the sea on the pebbles around an old windmill. The restaurant serves good-value English, Greek and Chinese food and there's live music every night, as well as great views of aircraft landing and taking off at the airport. ⓐ East end of Nea Paralia, beyond the 'Club Strip' ⓣ 24270 21412 ⓛ 12.00–15.00, 20.00–02.00 daily

Roes ££ ❽ Greek music in a modern setting. ⓐ Just off Plateia Papadiamantis (opposite the museum) ⓣ 24270 23306 ⓛ 21.00–02.00 daily

Arena £££ ❾ Dizzyingly expensive but authentically Greek – this is *the* place to go for a *bouzouki* music experience. ⓐ Nea Paralia, Ammoudia ⓣ 69473 76489 (mobile) ⓛ 22.00–02.00 daily (July & Aug)

CLUBS & MUSIC BARS

Old Port House Bar A fun atmosphere prevails at this Brit-run bar in the port, which serves a good range of cocktails, draught beers and ciders. ⓐ Old Port ⓣ 24270 23711 ⓛ 10.00–02.00 daily

Pure White couches and purple cushions under palm trees or beside the sea, with sounds to chill to. ⓐ Nea Paralia, Ammoudia ⓣ 69743 59626 or 69754 08540 (mobile) ⓛ 22.00–02.00 daily (July & Aug)

Red Morocco Harem-style décor makes this seaside nightspot stand out, with its red cushions and couches and mirror-walled bar. ⓐ Nea Paralia, Ammoudia ⓛ 22.00–02.00 daily (July & Aug)

Koukounaries

Koukounaries is probably Skiathos' best beach resort – and indeed one of the best in all of Greece – with a huge, south-facing crescent of golden sand, dazzling turquoise sea and lush green pine forest that comes almost down to the water's edge. Watersports abound, and the beach is dotted with café-bars that open at the beginning of the holiday season and only close when the last holidaymakers have flown home. The beach is kept spotlessly clean, and the sea is transparently clear. Having said all this, Koukounaries is not a resort for anyone seeking much more than an idyllic beach holiday; the resort consists of little more than a handful of small to medium-sized hotels, with half a dozen bars and restaurants scattered along the main road and a few small shops that purvey holiday essentials such as beach toys, sunblock and swimwear.

Beyond Koukounaries is Cape Tourkovigla, the southwestern tip of Skiathos. There's no public transport beyond Koukounaries – bus stop 26, at the west end of the beach, is the end of the line from Skiathos Town, and the island's main coast road runs out of asphalt at Aghia Eleni, about 1.5 km (1 mile) north of Koukounaries. To travel beyond this point, you really need a 4WD vehicle or a trail bike. Just inland from the beach is Koukounaries' famous 'lagoon' (see pages 27–8 & 30) – a brackish lake that drains into the sea at the west end of the beach – and 15 minutes' walk westward, to the other side of Cape Tourkovigla, brings you to the Big and Small Banana beaches.

FLIES IN THE OINTMENT

Koukounaries is one of the most beautiful spots in Greece, but there is trouble in paradise. In summer, the mosquitoes that breed in its famous lagoon can be a real pest after dark. Repellents to keep them off are readily available locally, and if your hotel room is not already equipped with an electric mosquito deterrent device it's well worth buying one from one of the local shops.

BEACHES

Ambelakia

Walk west from bus stop 26 and the car park at the west end of Koukounaries beach on the dirt road that leads to Banana beach, then turn left on an even smaller dirt track (you'll see the signpost pointing to Ambelakia about 90 m/100 yds after leaving the car park) to walk over the headland of Tourkovigla to Ambelakia beach, a tiny crescent of powdery white sand hemmed in by pine-covered slopes. There's one small cantina here, serving basic meals and drinks and renting loungers and umbrellas, but no other services.

Big Banana

Big Banana was once a nudist beach, but is no longer – although it's still acceptable to go topless here. It's just south of Small Banana (see page 28) and is separated from it by a narrow, rocky headland that you can scramble across. The water is deliciously clear and warm, and the sand is perfect. Big Banana has somewhat better services than Small Banana, including lifeguards in high season, toilets and showers, two self-service beach cantinas, and an array of watersports including kayaks, banana rides and pedalos.

Koukounaries

Some sources rate Koukounaries as one of the finest beaches in the Mediterranean. It is certainly right up there with the best – more than a kilometre (½ mile) of stunning golden sand, with all the facilities you could want, including showers, spotless toilets, changing cubicles, lifeguards (in high season only), a string of cheerful beach bars that sell cold drinks, snacks and light meals from dawn until dusk, and half a dozen watersports outfits offering kayaks, waterskiing, parascending and more. The beach is kept extremely clean, and its sheltered, shallow waters make it ideal for children of all ages. Koukounaries is also extraordinary for its wooded lagoon, which attracts nature lovers seeking to lay eyes on its myriad migratory birds, including the kingfisher, or to gaze on its flowering meadows. The best seasons for birdwatching at this serene spot are spring and autumn. Access is from bus stop 26, at the west end of the beach, or bus stop 23, near the east end. At the east end of the beach, a channel of clear water flows between the sea and the Koukounaries lagoon, forming a natural harbour where yachts and leisure boats are moored, and which is crossed by a wooden footbridge.

Small Banana

It's a bit of a hike from bus stop 26, at the west end of Koukounaries beach, to the double bay that is officially called Ormos Krassa, but which has for years been better known by its nickname Banana beach. But for some dedicated naturists in search of a perfect all-over tan, the trek is worth it. A 20-minute walk along a dirt track, following the signs to 'Banana' (as the beaches have been known since the first nudists arrived here in the 1970s), takes you through olive groves to two bays of golden sand, separated by a narrow, rocky headland, that were hippy heaven in the years before Skiathos became a holiday hotspot. These days, Small Banana – the northernmost and smaller of the two bays – is the last stretch of beach on the island, and perfect for sunbathing in relative privacy. There's one small summer cantina, which serves snacks and cold drinks and rents sunloungers and umbrellas, but there are no other services here.

Troulos

About 3 km (2 miles) east of Koukounaries (get off at bus stop 19 or 20), Troulos is a busy little south-facing beach set between rocky, pine-strewn headlands. On the horizon are the misty blue hills of Evia, and in the middle of the bay, not far offshore, the tiny, uninhabited Touranes islands add interest to the view. Two small freshwater streams flow down to the beach here, creating green pools that provide miniature havens for frogs, dragonflies and terrapins. Troulos also has rather more than its fair share of good places to eat, with no fewer than four restaurants right on the beach.

⬛ *The beach at Koukounaries is rated one of the best in Greece*

THINGS TO SEE & DO

Horse riding

Explore the hinterland of Skiathos on horseback from this friendly, professionally operated riding centre, which has a troop of eight locally bred part-Arab horses and two gentle donkeys for younger children.
Skiathos Riding Center ⓐ Bus stop 25, Koukounaries ⓣ 24270 49750 ⓦ www.skiathos-horse-riding.gr ⓛ 09.00–12.00, 15.00–18.00 daily

Island cruises

Cruise boats leave daily in summer from Koukounaries harbour, at the east end of the beach, sailing clockwise around the island, with stops for swimming and lunch at Mandraki, and Megalos Aselinos, on the north coast with views of deserted Kastro from the sea. Tickets are sold on board, but in high season it is advisable to make a reservation the evening before you intend to go.
Excursion boats ⓐ Koukounaries harbour, bus stop 21 ⓛ Depart 09.40, return 17.00

Lagoon

The renowned Koukounaries lagoon is almost unique in the Greek islands. It's a long, broad expanse of brackish, jade-green water, linked to the sea by a narrow channel at its western end. Between the lagoon and the beach is an expanse of thick pine woodland, and on its north side is a wide spread of reedbeds and wild-flower meadows that is colourful all year round and attracts dozens of butterflies. Kingfishers can often be seen on the lake, and in spring and autumn it provides a refuge for many migratory waterbirds.

Watersports

Koukounaries has the best choice of watersports on Skiathos, ranging from waterskiing and wakeboarding to parascending, canoeing and kayaking. Motorboats and jet-skis can also be rented. There are at least four watersports rental kiosks dotted along the beach every summer.

◉ The lagoon at Koukounaries is a protected nature reserve

Operators change from year to year, and reservations are not taken by phone – your best bet is to make your arrangements the day before.

Astir Ski Club rents 'UFOs', rubber rings, waterskis and wakeboards, and all safety equipment. ⓐ West end of Koukounaries beach ⓣ 24270 23221 ⓛ 09.00–dusk daily

Diolettas Boat Rental rents motorboats by the day and also rents 'sea-taxis'. ⓐ Midway along Koukounaries beach ⓣ 24270 49469 ⓛ 09.00–dusk daily

TAKING A BREAK

BARS & CAFÉS
Half a dozen summer beach bar-restaurants are strung out along the boardwalk that runs along Koukounaries beach, so you are never far from a cold beer or soft drink, a salad, a pizza or a light lunch.

Banana Beach Bar ££ Serving cold drinks and snacks to Banana beach aficionados from morning until after sunset, with comfortable chairs and couches under the pine trees. ⓐ Big Banana beach ⓛ 11.00–20.00 daily

Banana Paradise ££ Laid-back, self-service beach bar serving snacks and exotic cocktails, beer and soft drinks. ⓐ Big Banana beach ⓛ 11.00–21.00 daily

RESTAURANTS
Strofilia £ Outdoor tables in shady gardens (which it shares with the Strofilia Hotel, of which the restaurant is part) and a menu that comprises lots of grilled meat, salads and pizzas. It also has Internet access. ⓐ Bus stop 24, Koukounaries ⓣ 22071 42251 ⓛ 12.00–15.00, 18.00–22.00 daily

Apaloosa Bar Taverna ££ Located near bus stop 18, this is a friendly traditional taverna presided over in grand style by the impressive figure of Captain Nikos. The lamb *kleftiko* is particularly delicious. ⓐ Bus stop 18, Troulos 🕐 11.00–22.00 daily

The Big Bad Wolf ££ Meaty grills and big salads are the signature dishes of this restaurant under the pine trees. ⓐ Bus stop 23, Koukounaries ⓣ 24270 24185 🕐 12.00–15.00, 19.00–23.00 daily

Elia's ££ Probably the poshest place to eat in Koukounaries, part of the Mandraki Village Hotel. ⓐ Mandraki Village Hotel, bus stop 23, Koukounaries ⓣ 24270 49303 ⓦ www.mandraki-skiathos.gr 🕐 12.00–15.00, 19.00–22.00 daily

Green Meadow Taverna ££ Traditional Greek menu in a former farmhouse with tables set on lawns that are indeed quite green in spring, though somewhat parched in summer. Children's playground. Five minutes' walk from Troulos beach. ⓐ Bus stop 19, Troulos ⓣ 24270 49285 🕐 12.00–15.00, 19.00–23.00 daily

Strofilia Restaurant ££ Serves charcoal-grilled meat dishes, pizzas, pasta and salads at outdoor tables under pine trees, opposite the lagoon but beside the main road. ⓐ Bus stop 24, Koukounaries ⓣ 24270 42251 🕐 12.00–15.00, 19.00–22.00 daily

Taverna Troulos ££ This is an attractive taverna with tables under awnings beside the beach and a menu that ranges from grilled fish and salads to oven-cooked dishes such as *moussaka* and lemon chicken. ⓐ Troulos beach, bus stop 20 ⓣ 24270 49255 ⓦ www.troulos.gr 🕐 12.00–22.00 daily

Agia Paraskevi

Approximately midway along the south coast of Skiathos – roughly
equidistant from Skiathos Town to the east and Koukounaries to the
west – Platanias Bay (Ormos Platanias) is sheltered by the headland of
Cape Tsirimokokalo on its west side and the Kanapitsa peninsula, which
juts southward into the Aegean, on its east side.

The small resort of Agia Paraskevi faces southwest across this
sheltered bay, with pine-covered headlands on either side, and is the
nucleus of a string of mini-resorts stretching from Poros on the west
side of Platanias Bay to Vromolimnos on the west side of the Kanapitsa
peninsula. This stretch of Skiathos' south coast offers an array of beach
sports ranging from bungee jumping to waterskiing, and a choice of fine
sandy beaches.

BEACHES

Agia Paraskevi

Agia Paraskevi is the only beach on the island that truly rivals
Koukounaries, with almost 1.5 km (1 mile) of clean yellow sand.
You won't be alone here in high season, as it is lined virtually from end
to end with sunloungers and umbrellas. Facilities include toilets,
showers, lifeguards (high season only) and a small drinks kiosk. At the
west end of the beach, the posh Skiathos Princess Hotel rents not only
umbrellas but also luxurious pavilion-style beach tents and has a
stylish beach café-bar.

Kolios

Kolios beach, just east of Agia Paraskevi and separated from it by an
unclimbable rocky headland, is smaller and less crowded than its
neighbour but has equally attractive golden sand. The beach has plenty
of sunloungers and umbrellas, but there are no watersports, showers,
toilets or other beach facilities. There is one modest taverna, however,
which serves a reasonable choice of meals, snacks and drinks.

● *The sheltered bay at Agia Paraskevi*

> ## SUNLOUNGERS AND UMBRELLAS
> The municipality of Skiathos island provides sunloungers and umbrellas on all the south-coast beaches. At the time of writing, the going rate for one umbrella and two sunloungers was €8 per day. On most beaches, the cafés and tavernas also provide sunloungers and umbrellas free or at nominal cost for patrons.

Poros
Poros beach, about 1 km (½ mile) west of Agia Paraskevi, at bus stop 17, has a few tavernas and places to stay beside a stretch of sand beneath wooded slopes. It is great for those looking for a quieter holiday. For a wider choice of places to eat and things to do, head east to Agia Paraskevi or west to Koukounaries.

Vromolimnos
Vromolimnos, on the west side of the Kanapitsa peninsula and about 20 minutes' walk from bus stop 13 on the main road, has less sand than Agia Paraskevi, but makes up for it with a choice of activities, including waterskiing, wakeboarding and bungee jumping, as well as what is probably the loudest daytime and after-dark party scene on the island.

THINGS TO SEE & DO

Bungee jumping
Bungee jumping from a gantry above the beach is available for bolder spirits at Vromolimnos beach.

Watersports
There are two watersports outfits at Agia Paraskevi, both nameless and both renting pedalos, kayaks and windsurfing boards and rigs, and offering waterskiing, wakeboarding and inflatable rides. A full range of watersports is also available at Vromolimnos.

◗ *Enjoy watery thrills and spills at Agia Paraskevi*

TAKING A BREAK

Boubounakia £ Small snack bar serving *souvlaki*, *gyros*, pitta, snacks and cold drinks, next to the Iguana Pool Bar. ⓐ Bus stop 16, Agia Paraskevi ⓣ 24270 49312 ⓛ 11.00–22.00 daily

Iguana Pool Bar £ Part of the small Roula Apartments complex on the inland side of the main road, Iguana offers poolside loungers, drinks, snacks and light meals. ⓐ Bus stop 16, Agia Paraskevi ⓣ 24270 49312 ⓛ 10.00–23.00 daily

Infinity Blue £££ Sophisticated restaurant serving excellent seafood, including fresh spiny lobster (*astakos*), and an array of mouthwatering fish. ⓐ Bus stop 15, above Kolios beach ⓣ 24270 49750 ⓦ www.infinityblue.gr ⓛ 12.00–15.00, 19.00–23.00 daily

Princess Ammos £££ The bar-restaurant of the luxurious Skiathos Princess Hotel serves light meals, cold drinks and cocktails and, with its crew of waiters dressed in immaculate white, it is the island's smartest beach restaurant. ⓐ West end of Agia Paraskevi beach ⓣ 24270 49731 ⓦ www.skiathosprincess.com ⓛ 10.00–20.00 daily

Tzaneria (Nostos)

Tzaneria (also known as Nostos) is small but relatively uncrowded, with a curve of clean but coarse sand and pebbles, and water that is dazzlingly blue even by the high standards of Skiathos. Tzaneria does not have showers, toilets or lifeguards on the beach, but it does have a scuba-diving centre and a watersports centre, both at the east end of the beach, and a rather good taverna and beach bar midway along the beach (part of the Nostos Village Holiday Resort, which occupies a section of the hillside immediately above the beach). Around 1 km (½ mile) south of Tzaneria – a steep hike over a hilly headland, then down a flight of steps back to sea level – is Kanapitsa, a pleasantly secluded and surprisingly uncrowded bay overlooked by two upmarket hotels and with a small watersports centre and one attractive taverna.

There are reasonably priced water-taxis from both Kanapitsa and Tzaneria to Skiathos Town, leaving hourly from 09.00 and taking around ten minutes (the fare costs around three times as much as the bus to/from Tzaneria, but for those without a hired car or bike the water-taxi saves the hike from bus stop 12 to Kanapitsa).

THINGS TO SEE & DO

Scuba diving

Dolphin Diving offers sample dives and qualification courses for beginners, as well as dives for experienced divers, including cave dives, drift dives and night dives. More experienced divers are also catered for at the Octopus Diving Center in Skiathos Town (see page 22).
ⓐ Dolphin Diving Center, Nostos Village Holiday Resort, Tzaneria
ⓣ 24270 21599 ⓦ www.ddiving.gr ⓛ 09.00–19.00 daily (May–late Oct)

Tennis

The tennis court at the Nostos Village Holiday Resort, immediately inland from Tzaneria beach, can be rented by the hour by non-residents.
ⓐ Nostos Village Holiday Resort ⓦ www.nostosvillage.gr ⓛ 10.00–18.00

⬥ *The tranquil setting of the water-taxi landing point at Kanapitsa*

TAKING A BREAK

Nostos Beach Bar £ Adjoining the Nafsika Beach Restaurant, this café-bar serves cold drinks and snacks all day. ⓐ Nostos Village Holiday Resort Ⓦ www.nostosvillage.gr Ⓛ 11.00–20.00 daily

Kanapitsa Taverna ££ The only place to eat on Kanapitsa beach, but despite having a monopoly, this taverna does not rest on its laurels but serves a good choice of seafood, meat dishes and salads. It also offers a water-taxi service to and from Skiathos Town. ⓐ Kanapitsa beach Ⓣ 24270 21191 Ⓛ 11.00–22.00 daily

Nafsika Beach Restaurant ££ This adequate (but not inspired) restaurant is your only option for a full meal at Tzaneria. ⓐ Nostos Village Holiday Resort Ⓦ www.nostosvillage.gr Ⓛ 12.00–15.00, 19.00–23.00 daily

⬤ *The clear waters of Skiathos are excellent for snorkelling*

Achladies

Roughly 2 km (1½ miles) northeast of Tzaneria (reached by bus stop 10 at the west end and bus stop 9 at the east end, or by water-taxi), Achladies is a long sweep of yellow sand that faces southeast towards the small islands of Tsougriaki and Tsougria. Like all the south-coast beaches, it is lined with sunloungers and umbrellas in summer, and it has a reasonable choice of places to eat, drink and stay. Lifeguards are on duty in summer, there are showers and toilets on the beach, and there is a watersports centre.

Though it is far from uncrowded in July and August, Achladies has one of the best locations on the island – the other beaches of the south coast are easily accessible by boat, car and bus, and the shops, restaurants and nightlife of Skiathos Town are also easy to get to.

THINGS TO SEE & DO

Parascending, wakeboarding, boat rental and waterskiing are all available here and a range of water toys, including various inflatable rides, kayaks and canoes, can be rented on the beach. ⓐ Achladies Watersports, Achladies beach 🕒 10.00–18.00 daily

TAKING A BREAK

Maniatis Garden ££ Beach bar and restaurant with veranda overlooking the bay, midway along Achladies beach. ⓐ Achladies beach ☎ 24270 24455 ⓦ www.maniatisgarden.gr 🕒 11.00–22.00 daily

Taverna Paradise and Bar ££ Claims to offer 'the best Greek night in Skiathos' with live music and traditional dancing every Thursday night in summer. The rest of the week it serves a good choice of grills, salads and seafood. ⓐ East end of Achladies beach ☎ 24270 22122 🕒 12.00–15.00, 17.00–24.00 daily

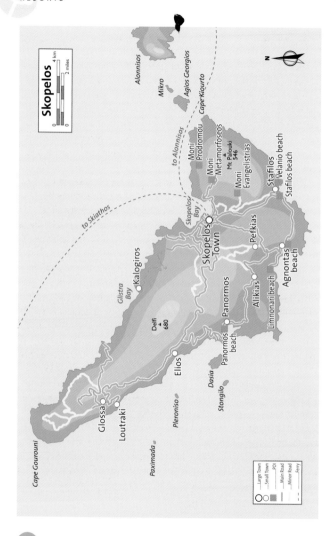

Skopelos

Alonnisos

Mikro

Agios Georgios

Cape Kiourto

to Alonnisos

Moni Prodromou

Moni Metamorfoseos

Mt Palouki 546

Moni Evangelistrias

Staflos

Velanio beach

Staflos beach

Skopelos Bay

to Skiathos

Skopelos Town

Pefkias

Kalogiros

Glistra Bay

Delfi 680

Panormos

Alikias

Agnontas beach

Limnonari beach

Panormos beach

Elios

Dasia

Stongilo

Pleroniso

Glossa

Loutraki

Paximada

Cape Gourouni

Large Town
Small Town
POI
Main Road
Minor Road
Ferry

Skopelos

Skopelos is slightly larger than its neighbours Skiathos and Alonnisos, and is more mountainous, with a ridge of steeply sloping hills, covered by woods, orchards and vineyards, which runs the length of the island, rising to its highest point, Mount Delfi, 680 m (2,230 ft) above sea level. Steep cliffs plunge down to the sea in many places, making much of its coastline inaccessible. Unlike Skiathos, Skopelos has no huge sweeps of golden sand. Instead, it has a plethora of small, white-pebble coves and bays framed by pine-covered slopes.

This tranquil island has experienced a considerable tourism boom in recent years, particularly since the massive global success of the *Mamma Mia!* film, parts of which were filmed here. Its pretty island capital, Skopelos Town, is very lively in summer, with bustling cafés along its waterfront and plenty of nightlife. Skopelos Town stands on a bay that forms a fine natural harbour on the north coast of the island, and its streets of whitewashed houses with roofs of grey-stone slabs and wooden balconies are overlooked by a cluster of age-old churches. Panaghitsa tou Pyrgou, perched on a crag above the harbour, is the most prominent of these, but there are more than 100 churches and chapels tucked away in the steep, narrow streets of the labyrinthine old quarter. Skopelos Town has grown rapidly since 2003, when its harbour was expanded, with a string of new hotels stretching along the beach east of the harbour and many new houses on the hillsides above the old village.

The island is around 16 km (10 miles) in length from north to south, and roughly 10 km (6 miles) across at its widest point. Glossa, perched on a hillside high above the sea near the island's northern tip, is Skopelos' only other village of any size, and has its own harbour at Loutraki. It is a typical traditional Greek hilltop village with lovely whitewashed island houses. Skopelos' third harbour village is Agnontas, on the south coast – a sleepy little port that is normally used only by yachts, fishing boats and day-trip boats, but where ferries and hydrofoils occasionally call.

BEACHES

From Skopelos Town, going south and then up the west coast, the main beaches to try are listed below:

Skopelos Town

Skopelos Town has a stretch of shingly beach that extends eastward from the new harbour. Loungers and umbrellas are available, and there's one café-bar on the beach as well as numerous others on the opposite side of the beach road.

Stafilos

Stafilos, 4 km (2½ miles) south of Skopelos Town, on the southeast coast of the island, is a deep blue bay with a pebbly beach and a handful of places to eat and drink. As the closest beach to Skopelos Town, it is crowded in July and August.

Velanio

A five-minute walk eastward from Stafilos, over the rocky headland of Cape Stafilos, brings you to Velanio, an even smaller pebbly cove with no facilities other than a summer cantina selling cold drinks and snacks. Unlike other Skopelos beaches, Velanio still attracts a few determined nudists in search of an all-over tan.

Agnontas

Agnontas is not much more than a row of houses, tavernas and guesthouses built around a small, crescent-shaped harbour that is used mainly by yachts and fishing boats. The minuscule beach is clean and pebbly.

Limnonari

Limnonari, less than 1 km (½ mile) north of Agnontas, is a long curve of white pebbles and coarse sand beneath steep, pine-covered slopes, and the water here is almost always calm and very clean.

● *Skopelos Town has a fine natural harbour*

Panormos

Panormos, on a sheltered, west-facing bay midway up the west coast of the island (18 km/11 miles from Skopelos Town), is the nearest thing Skopelos has to a purpose-built holiday resort, with a pebbly beach and a series of smaller sandy coves on either side of the main beach. Watersports, including waterskiing and windsurfing, are on offer, and kayaks, pedalos and small motorboats can be rented.

THINGS TO SEE & DO

Bakratsa Museum

This recently opened folk museum showcases traditional ceremonial island dress of yesteryear. It's located 100 m (110 yds) up a narrow lane, across from the central waterfront. ☎ 24240 22940 🕐 11.00–13.00, 18.00–22.00 daily ❶ Admission charge

Folklore Museum

Clearly signposted from several points along the harbour esplanade, the Folklore Museum contains an interesting collection of traditional costumes, folk art, pottery and embroidery. ⓐ Harzistamati, Skopelos Town ☎ 24240 23494 🕐 10.30–22.00 daily ❶ Admission charge

Moni Evangelistrias

On the slopes of Mount Palouki, high above Skopelos Town, stands the 18th-century monastery of Moni Evangelistrias. Its splendid interior is concealed behind high, fortress-like walls, and it's surrounded by thick woodland. It's worth visiting just for the view from here. ⓐ 2 km (1½ miles) east of Skopelos Town 🕐 08.00–13.00, 17.00–18.00 daily

Motorboat rental

Rent a motorboat and discover hidden bays and coves only accessible by sea. Boats fitted with sun canopies and cool-boxes for drinks and snacks can be rented from **Holiday Islands** (ⓐ Panormos beach, Skopelos Town ☎ 24240 24788) by the day or week without a special licence.

⬤ One of the many picturesque bays on Skopelos

⬢ *A typical, balconied house in Skopelos Town's old quarter*

Cruises to the National Marine Park of Alonnisos

Boats leave daily from Skopelos Town for the National Marine Park of Alonnisos, around 90 minutes from Skopelos, where the waters around an archipelago of uninhabited islands provide a refuge for endangered monk seals, dolphins and even whales, as well as several species of rare birds. Cruises include stops for swimming, a picnic lunch and a visit to the tiny monastery on Kyra Panagia island. Boats leave daily in summer, departing at around 09.00 and returning around 19.00.

Kassandra Cruises ⓐ Skopelos Town harbour ❶ 69726 98114 (mobile) ⓦ www.kassandracruises.com

Panther Cruises ⓐ Skopelos Town harbour ❶ 69456 53631 (mobile)

Walking

British expat Heather Parsons leads guided walks through Skopelos' beautiful hills and woodlands. Itineraries range from gentle rambles through Skopelos Town and the surrounding countryside to more challenging longer hikes. ❶ 24240 24022, 69452 49328 (mobile) ⓦ www.skopelos-walks.com

TAKING A BREAK

BARS & CAFÉS

Blue Sea £ Café-bar beside the harbour, with high-speed Internet access and DJs playing music in the evening. ⓐ West end of Skopelos Town harbour ❶ 24240 23010 ❶ 10.00–23.00 daily

Obreles £ Beach bar just east of the harbour, serving cold drinks, cocktails, smoothies and fruit juices. Free sunloungers and umbrellas for patrons and a DJ from 17.30 to 20.30 every evening. ⓐ Skopelos Town beach ❶ 69729 33781 (mobile) ❶ 10.00–20.30 daily

Pablo's £ Skopelos Town's newest and trendiest café-bar, with a good wine list as well as beers and cocktails. ⓐ Skopelos Town harbour ❶ 24240 24804 ❶ 10.00–02.00 daily

RESTAURANTS

Platanos £ Excellent value day or night, this authentically Greek restaurant serves huge platters of grilled meat and large salads under the shade of a 100-year-old plane tree. ⓐ Plateia Platanos, Skopelos Town ① 24240 23067 ⌚ 08.30–24.00 daily

Englezos ££ Englezos serves traditional island cuisine using locally sourced, seasonal produce. ⓐ Skopelos Town harbour ① 24240 22230 ⌚ 12.00–15.00, 19.00–23.00 daily

Molos ££ Excellent grilled seafood including spiny lobster, sea bream, sardines, red mullet and more. ⓐ Skopelos Town harbour ① 24240 22551 ⌚ 12.00–15.00, 19.00–23.00 daily

Terpsi ££ Traditional-style taverna serving grilled meat and oven-cooked dishes such as *giouvetsi* and *moussaka*. ⓐ Panormos Road, 4 km (2½ miles) from Skopelos Town centre ① 24240 22053 ⌚ 12.00–15.00, 19.00–24.00 daily

AFTER DARK

Nightlife on Skopelos centres on the string of music bars along the coast road just south of the ferry harbour, behind the beach. These include:

Bamboo £ Friendly bar serving good cocktails and snacks and playing ethnic and ambient sounds after sundown. ⓐ Harbour beach road, Skopelos Town ⌚ 11.00–02.00 daily

Karavi £££ You can't miss this hottest of Skopelos nightspots, built into and around the wooden hull of a derelict wooden schooner beached beside the harbour road. This is the nearest thing Skopelos has to a club scene, and drinks prices are sky-high. ⓐ Harbour beach road, Skopelos Town ⌚ 18.00–02.00 daily

⬤ *Agios Ioannis chapel near Glossa will be familiar to* Mamma Mia! *film fans*

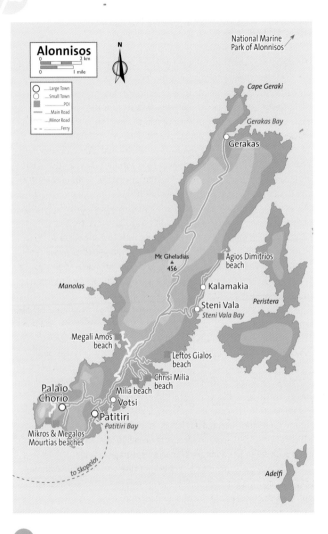

National Marine
Park of Alonnisos

Alonnisos

0   2 km
0   1 mile

N

○ ....Large Town
○ ....Small Town
■ ....POI
— ....Main Road
— ....Minor Road
- - - ....Ferry

Cape Geraki

Gerakas Bay

Gerakas

Agios Dimitrios
beach

Mt Gheladias
▲
456

Manolas

Kalamakia

Steni Vala
Steni Vala Bay

Peristera

Megali Amos
beach

Leftos Gialos
beach

Chrisi Milia
beach

Palaio
Chorio

Milia beach

Votsi

Patitiri
Patitiri Bay

Mikros & Megalos
Mourtias beaches

to Skopelos

Adelfi

Alonnisos

This long, thin island – around 16 km (10 miles) from north to south and less than 3 km (2 miles) across at its widest point – is perfect for people looking for a peaceful holiday in pretty surroundings.

Although less than 30 minutes away by ferry from Skopelos, its nearest neighbour, the pace of life here is slower and tourism is much less developed. This is partly because Alonnisos is just that little bit further away and takes a little longer to reach – but it's well worth the effort. Pine-covered hills slope down to a coastline that is dotted with small beaches separated by rocky headlands, and the water around the island is amazingly clear and vividly blue.

Alonnisos has only two real villages, plus a scattering of tiny beach settlements. The island's original main village, Palaio Chorio ('Old Village'), stands high in the hills near the south end of the island. It was heavily damaged by an earthquake in 1965, and most of its inhabitants moved to new homes at Patitiri, the island's main harbour, where you'll find most of the island's smaller hotels and guesthouses, restaurants, shops, travel agencies and car- and bike-rental agencies.

Patitiri is also the port for ferries and hydrofoils to and from Skiathos, Skopelos and Volos, on the mainland. In recent years, however, Palaio Chorio has come back to life, with foreigners and Athenian Greeks moving in to renovate dilapidated old houses as holiday homes and art studios.

Alonnisos is surrounded by an archipelago of smaller islands, which are mostly uninhabited. These are home to a number of rare and endangered birds, plants and mammals, and the islands and the waters around them are protected by the National Marine Park of Alonnisos, which is one of the largest nature reserves in Europe and home to a number of rare and endangered species (see pages 61–2).

Alonnisos has a surprisingly active nightlife, with a handful of music bars, *bouzouki* clubs (a *bouzouki* is similar to a mandolin) and dance clubs. It also offers a plethora of activities, from yoga and watercolour painting classes to windsurfing, walking and scuba diving.

MONK SEALS

The monk seal (*Monachus monachus*) is one of the world's rarest mammals – there are fewer than 500 of them. Around 250 live in Greek seas, and the islands of the National Marine Park of Alonnisos are home to around 50 adult seals. Monk seals have suffered from loss of habitat and pollution, and fishing has severely depleted their food supplies. They are no longer hunted, but in the past their skins were used to make the traditional curly-toed sandals worn by the islanders of Alonnisos and Skyros.

Monk seals rest and raise their young in the sea-caves of the uninhabited islands around Alonnisos, which are off-limits to visitors. Around eight seal pups are born in the caves each year, and as monk seals can live to 45 years old, the population is slowly growing. The Hellenic Society for the Study and Protection of the Monk Seal (**MOm** ① 21052 22888, 24240 66350 (local branch) ⓦ www.mom.gr) monitors these seals and campaigns for their protection. To find out how to support MOm's efforts, visit its website. The society also has an information centre in the port of Patitiri. ⓛ 10.00–20.00 daily (summer)

BEACHES

Alonnisos' coastline is studded with small beaches, separated by rocky, pine-covered headlands and sloping down into amazingly clear turquoise water. The most popular beaches, clearly, are those closest to Patitiri, most of which have at least one seasonal café-bar and ranks of pay-by-the-day sunloungers and umbrellas. The east-coast beaches get less crowded as you head north, while on the west coast, there are even more secluded coves that can only be reached on foot or by boat. Most beaches on Alonnisos are of clean white pebbles, but there are some sandy stretches, too. The list that follows on pages 59–60 covers the beaches from the south and up the east coast.

⬤ *The amazing colour of the sea in the famous 'blue cave', Alonnisos*

⬤ *One of the few unrenovated old houses in Palaio Chorio*

Megalos Mourtias

Steep cliffs loom either side of Megalos Mourtias, which is the nearest place for a swim if you're staying in (or visiting) Palaio Chorio. It's about a 30-minute walk, and the beach is pebbly, but once you're in the water the sea bottom is sandy. There are tavernas beside the beach, among olive groves. The quieter **Mikros Mourtias** is also accessible from Palaio Chorio.

Patitiri Bay

This stretch of white pebbles just west of Patitiri's harbour isn't the best beach on the island – but it's certainly the most conveniently located. The water is clean, and there's a row of cafés and restaurants right on the beach. It's perfect for a pre-lunch dip while you're in Patitiri. There are no showers, sunloungers or umbrellas, however.

Votsi

Votsi is virtually a suburb of Patitiri, set on a pretty natural harbour with a yacht marina, a handful of seaside tavernas and a tiny (and usually crowded) stretch of white pebbles.

Milia

Around five minutes' drive north of Patitiri, Milia is another white-pebble beach between two pine-covered headlands, with a small summer cantina serving snacks and cold drinks, and with a flotilla of floating inflatable slides and trampolines to keep children entertained.

SEA URCHINS

Beware of sea urchins, which lurk on the rocks just below the waterline on many beaches. Fortunately, these black, spiky creatures are easy to see and avoid. Their orange insides (eaten raw) are also a favourite Greek snack – on any beaches, heaps of empty sea-urchin shells show where locals have enjoyed an impromptu picnic.

Chrisi Milia

Chrisi Milia, 4 km (3 miles) north of Patitiri, is one of the few sandy beaches on Alonnisos.

Leftos Gialos

This long pebble beach surrounded by olive groves is one of the prettiest on the island, with radiantly clear water, and is usually uncrowded. There are two or three small summer tavernas, but no other facilities.

Steni Vala

On the north shore of a narrow, fjord-like bay, Steni Vala is a quiet little fishing village that was once a pirates' lair. A row of fish tavernas stands along a quayside where yachts and fishing boats are moored, and there are small pebble beaches either side of the village. There's a good choice of watersports, including windsurfing, kayaking and scuba diving.

Kalamakia

About 3 km (2 miles) north of Steni Vala, this minute fishing harbour has a tiny pebble beach and a clutch of good seafood restaurants, making it a pleasant place to stop for lunch.

Agios Dimitrios

This long pebble beach faces the sparsely inhabited island of Peristera, on the other side of a deep blue channel through which yachts and cruisers pass on their way to the nearby National Marine Park of Alonnisos. There are sunloungers and umbrellas on the beach, beside a couple of tavernas and small guesthouses, but this is the largest and most uncrowded beach on the east coast.

THINGS TO SEE & DO

Folklore Museum of the Northern Sporades

This well-designed little museum contains three separate exhibitions: old-fashioned craft tools and farming equipment; maritime paraphernalia and weapons from the island's piratical past; and a veritable arsenal of historical firearms and other exhibits relating to Greece's multiple wars of independence from 1821 to the 20th century.

ⓐ Patitiri Bay, above the beach and 200 m (195 yds) south of the harbour
ⓣ 24240 66250 ⓛ 10.00–21.00 (June–Sept) ⓘ Admission charge

Boating and kayaking

Many of Alonnisos' prettiest beaches are only accessible by sea, and motorboats with 15 hp and 30 hp outboard motors can be hired by the day from Patitiri. Agencies renting boats and kayaks include:

Albedo Travel ⓐ Patitiri harbour ⓣ 24240 65804
ⓦ www.albedotravel.com

Alonnisos Travel ⓐ Patitiri harbour ⓣ 24240 65188
ⓦ www.alonnisostravel.gr

Ikion Sport ⓐ Steni Vala harbour ⓣ 24240 65158 ⓦ www.ikiongroup.gr

National Marine Park of Alonnisos

A cruise through the waters of the National Marine Park of Alonnisos is a great day out. You may see dolphins or – if you are very lucky – one of the

△ *Head to Steni Vala Bay for excellent seafood*

monk seals that breed in the sea-caves of the uninhabited islands. Cruises also include stops for swimming, a visit to the island's famous 'blue cave', a picnic lunch and a visit to the tiny, picturesque monastery on Kyra Panagia island, north of Alonnisos. There is also a good chance of seeing rare Eleonora's falcons swooping and diving over the sea cliffs where they nest. Boats leave from Patitiri harbour daily in summer, departing at around 10.00 and returning around 18.30.

Ikos Travel ⓐ Patitiri harbour ⓣ 24240 65320 ⓦ www.ikostravel.com
Planitis Marine Park Cruises (Alonnisos Travel) ⓐ Patitiri harbour
ⓣ 24240 65188 ⓦ www.alonnisostravel.gr

Painting

Chris Hughes, a British artist who lives on Alonnisos, offers watercolour painting classes for novice and experienced painters at his studio on the hillside above Patitiri (ⓣ 24240 65124 ⓦ www.paintingalonissos.com).

⬥ *Rent a boat to see some of Alonnisos' otherwise inaccessible beaches*

Scuba diving

The waters around Alonnisos offer several good dives for all levels of experience, including wall and cave dives and at least one easily accessible wreck site.

Traditional House Museum

This sturdy old stone house at the end of Palaio Chorio's main street (above the church) is a lovingly restored family home, complete with portraits, photographs and old-fashioned household utensils and furniture. Outside, a plaque commemorates the nine villagers murdered by German troops on 15 August 1944, shortly before they retreated from Greece. ⓐ Plataia Iroon, Palaio Chorio
🕐 10.00–18.00 (June–Sept)

Walking

Alonnisos is hilly, but its hills are not challengingly steep (its highest point, Gheladias, is only 456 m/1,496 ft above sea level). Much of the countryside is shaded by thick pine woods, so exploring the island on foot is a real pleasure. A network of waymarked walking paths and old cobbled mule trails criss-crosses the hinterland, and you're never more than 10–15 minutes' walk from the coast for a cooling dip in the sea. Keen walkers should invest in a copy of *Alonnisos on Foot*, by local residents Bente Keller and Elias Tsoukanas (available from their shop, Gallery 5 in Palaio Chorio, and in shops in Patitiri).

Albedo Travel offers guided walking tours on Alonnisos and the islands of the National Marine Park of Alonnisos. ⓐ Patitiri harbour
☎ 24240 65804 🌐 www.albedotravel.com

A long-time resident of Alonnisos, British expat **Chris Browne** leads informative walking tours of the island for all fitness levels. See 🌐 www.alonnisoswalks.co.uk for full information.

Waltrand Helma Alberti leads 'herbal excursions' (duration two hours) during which you can learn to identify many of the wild healing herbs of the island. ☎ 24240 65916

Yoga

Yoga classes for beginners and experienced Hatha yoga and Ashtanga yoga practitioners are offered in Palaio Chorio and at several hotels around the island by **Kalithea Yoga** (❶ 24240 65513, 69759 30108 (mobile) Ⓦ www.kalithea.org ❸ Sessions: 10.15 & 18.00 Mon, Wed, Thur & Sun, and by appointment); massages are also available.

⬥ *A sightseeing boat moored off the island of Kyra Panagia, north of Alonnisos*

TAKING A BREAK

CAFÉS

Play Internet Café £ On Patitiri's main street (opposite the National Bank of Greece), this air-conditioned Internet café serves cold drinks and has blisteringly fast broadband access. ⓐ Patitiri ☎ 24240 66119 🕐 09.00–24.00 daily

Pleiades ££ The café-terrace of the Pleiades Hotel is the coolest place in town for drinks, snacks and light meals. ⓐ Above Patitiri harbour ☎ 24240 65235 🔲 www.pleiadeshotel.gr 🕐 09.00–24.00 daily

RESTAURANTS

Ouzerie Archipelagos £ This classic Greek establishment is a great place to enjoy *meze* (mixed Greek appetisers), seafood and the national aperitif, *ouzo*. ⓐ Patitiri ☎ 24240 65031 🕐 09.00–24.00 daily

Astrofegia ££ Attractive restaurant and bar on the edge of the old village, with a good range of traditional Greek dishes. ⓐ Palaio Chorio ☎ 24240 65182 🔲 www.alonissosastrofegia.com 🕐 19.00–24.00 daily

O Manolis ££ Rooftop tables with super views overlooking a tiny fishing harbour, from which the seafood comes fresh to your table. ⓐ Kalamakia, 3 km (2 miles) north of Steni Vala ☎ 24240 66262 🕐 12.00–15.00, 19.00–23.00 daily

I Tsitsiria ££ Located right beside the harbour, this amiable restaurant serves some of the best food in town. Good for lunch or dinner. ⓐ Waterfront, Patitiri ☎ 24240 65255 🕐 12.00–15.00, 18.00–23.00 daily

To Votsalo £££ Excellent traditional seafood restaurant by the sea, midway between Patitiri and Votsi. Not cheap, but the fish is very fresh. ⓐ Roussou Gialos, Patitiri (500 m/550 yds north of Patitiri harbour) ☎ 24240 65106 🕐 12.00–16.00, 19.00–24.00 daily

AFTER DARK

BARS

Club Stathmos This music bar on the harbour attracts hip young locals who move on to Boem (see Clubs) after 24.00. ⓐ Patitiri harbour ⓣ 24240 65888 ⓛ 12.00–02.00, DJ from 22.00

Sunset Café Bar £ This café and snack bar, set above the harbour, is open all day, but liveliest in the evening. An excellent place for sunset drinks. ⓐ Agios Onoufrios, Patitiri ⓣ 69375 18845 (mobile) ⓛ 12.00–01.00

LIVE MUSIC

Archontostasi £ Live traditional music, soft rock and jazz in a modern café-bar with superb sunset views. ⓐ 50 m (55 yds) east of the bus stop at Palaio Chorio ⓣ 24240 66310 ⓛ 19.00–01.00 (June–Sept)

Ta Kalamakia £ Excellent seaside fish taverna with live traditional Greek music on Sunday nights in high season. ⓐ Kalamakia ⓣ 24240 66400 ⓛ 12.00–15.00, 19.00–24.00; *bouzouki* nights: 21.00–23.00 Sun (July & Aug)

CLUBS

Boem A new venture by the owners of Club Armonia, now located next to the harbour. ⓐ Waterfront, Patitiri ⓣ 24240 66273 ⓛ 22.00–03.00 (June–Sept)

◗ *Fishing boats in the little harbour at Damouhari, the Pilion peninsula*

EXCURSIONS
Out & about

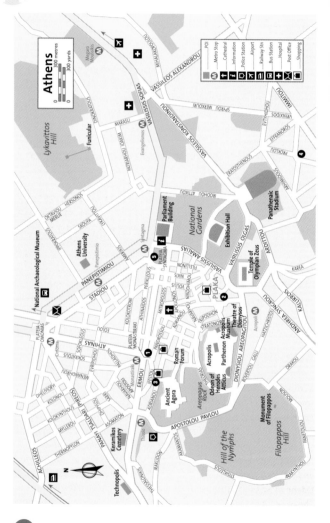

Athens

0   300 metres
0   300 yards

POI
Metro Stop
Cathedral
Information
Police Station
Airport
Railway Stn
Bus Station
Hospital
Post Office
Shopping

Lykavittos Hill

Funicular

Megaro Moussikis

Athens University

National Archaeological Museum

Parliament Building

National Gardens

Exhibition Hall

Temple of Olympian Zeus

Panathenaic Stadium

PLAKA

Roman Forum

Ancient Agora

Keramikos Cemetery

Technopolis

Odeon of Herodes Atticus

Acropolis

Parthenon

Acropolis Museum

Theatre of Dionysos

Areopagus Rock

Hill of the Nymphs

Monument of Filopappos

Filopappos Hill

APOSTOLOU PAVLOU

Athens

Greece's vibrant capital is surprisingly easy to get to from Skiathos, with a journey time of less than an hour to Athens' enviably modern airport. Athens has a better claim to represent the true face of Greece than any of the postcard-pretty resort islands – it is, after all, home to more than a third of the country's population. If you are looking to inject some urban excitement and a dose of culture into an otherwise indolent and sybaritic island holiday, there is no better place to do it.

Athens is an oddly exciting fusion of ancient and modern. It's a city that has been constantly reinventing itself for some 3,000 years, most recently with a massive overhaul in preparation for the 2004 Olympic Games, which endowed the city with a new airport and a portfolio of other improvements. Superb museums and ancient archaeological treasures that stand head and shoulders above those of any other European capital, and a unique cultural heritage are the most obvious of its attractions, but Athens is also just a great place in which to hang out and stroll around, with an open-air café seemingly at every street corner, enticing street markets to shop in, great places to eat and a selection of stylish new boutique hotels. Getting around has been made easier with the opening of an admirably clean and efficient metro system.

THINGS TO SEE & DO

Acropolis & Acropolis Museum

Towering above the city centre, the white marble columns of the **Parthenon** atop the steep-sided crag of the Acropolis are the ultimate symbol of the golden age of ancient Athens. Built during the late 5th century BC, after the city's triumph over the invading Persians, the temples of the Acropolis were dedicated to Athena, goddess of wisdom and victory and patron deity of Athens. Below the Acropolis stands the **Odeon of Herodes Atticus**, built during Roman times, and the huge **Theatre of Dionysos** – seating up to 15,000 people – where the works of

the great Greek dramatists were first performed. A ticket to the Acropolis also admits you to the new **Acropolis Museum**, which provides a superb showcase for many of the most important archaeological finds from the Acropolis. ⓐ Dionysiou Areopagitiou ⓣ Site and museum 21090 00901 ⓦ www.theacropolismuseum.gr ⓛ 08.00–20.00, closed Tues (Mar–Nov); 08.30–15.00 (Nov–Mar) ⓝ Acropoli ⓘ Entrance to the Ancient Agora & Roman Forum free with Acropolis ticket

Ancient Agora & Roman Forum

North of the Acropolis lies the Roman Forum, where toppled columns mark the sites of temples and public buildings laid out after the Roman conquest of Athens in the mid-2nd century AD. West of this site is the wider, grassy expanse of the Ancient Agora, which was the hub of the city for more than 1,000 years from the 6th century AD. ⓐ Adrianou ⓣ 21032 10185 ⓦ www.culture.gr ⓛ 08.30–20.00 (Apr–Oct); 08.00–17.30 (Nov–Mar) ⓝ Monastiraki ⓘ Entrance free with Acropolis ticket

Monastiraki & the 'Flea Markets'

Monastiraki sits at the northwest corner of the Plaka (see page 73). From this busy small square, you can plunge westward into the bustle of the Ifestou (or 'Old') Flea Market, a warren of streets crammed with shops selling street fashions, army surplus kits, antiques and curios, or head east to the 'New' Flea Market along Pandrossou, where shops and stalls sell smarter designer cottons and linens, gold and silver, and good-quality leather footwear, bags and accessories. ⓝ Monastiraki

National Archaeological Museum

This world-class museum houses the greatest treasures of Greece's many archaeological sites, including the gold 'Mask of Agamemnon' from ancient Mycenae, superb marble statues from the Classical and Hellenistic eras, bronzes, pottery and much more. ⓐ Patission 44 ⓣ 21082 17717 ⓦ www.namuseum.gr ⓛ 13.30–20.00 Mon, 08.30–20.00 Tues–Sun (Apr–Oct); 08.30–15.00 (Nov–Mar) ⓝ Victoria

⬥ Take the opportunity to visit the breathtaking Parthenon in Athens

⏶ View across the Ancient Agora, Athens

The Plaka

Between the Acropolis and Plateia Syntagma (the city's main square) lies the warren of narrow streets and old buildings known as the Plaka. It's crammed with souvenir shops, bars and restaurants, but it is still a living community, and a pleasant place to window-shop or stop for lunch or a drink at a pavement café. Follow the Plaka's main shopping street, Adrianou, which curves northwest through the quarter, to reach the city's other main ancient sites, the Ancient Agora and the Roman Forum.

TAKING A BREAK

Bairaktaris £ ❶   Grill restaurants cluster at the corner of Ermou and Plateia Monastiraki, with tables spilling out on to the street outside. Bairaktaris, which has been in business here for more than a century, is the best of these. ⓐ Plateia Monastiraki 2 ⓣ 21032 13036 ⓛ 11.00–24.00 daily

Diogenis ££ ❷   On the edge of the Plaka and convenient for the new Acropolis Museum, this bright modern restaurant and delicatessen specialises in free-range and organic food. An excellent spot for a light lunch or for buying supplies for a picnic beneath the Acropolis. ⓐ Selei 3, Plateia Lysokratous ⓣ 21032 47933 ⓛ 12.00–15.00, 19.00–24.00 daily

Milton's ££ ❸   Stylish, cool modern Greek restaurant located midway along Adrianou, conveniently close to the Ancient Agora and Roman Forum. ⓐ Adrianou 91 ⓣ 21032 49129 ⓛ 11.00–15.00, 19.00–24.00 daily

Spondi £££ ❹   A meal at Athens' finest restaurant will open your eyes to what Greek cooking can be when it tries. (It will also blow your budget.) Superb, imaginative and Michelin-acclaimed. ⓐ Pyrronos 5 ⓣ 21075 20658 ⓦ www.spondi.gr ⓛ 12.00–15.00, 20.00–24.00 daily

T-Palace £££ ❺   This smart new eating place offers Greek classics with a modern twist. ⓐ King George Palace Hotel, Plateia Syntagma ⓣ 21032 22210 ⓛ 12.00–24.00 daily

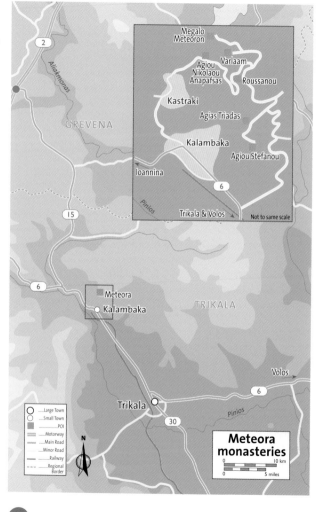

Megalo Meteoron
Varlaam
Agiou Nikolaou Anapafsas
Roussanou
Kastraki
Agias Triadas
Kalambaka
Agiou Stefanou
Ioannina
Trikala & Volos
Not to same scale

GREVENA

Aliakmonas

Pinios

TRIKALA

Meteora
Kalambaka

Volos

Trikala

Pinios

Large Town
Small Town
POI
Motorway
Main Road
Minor Road
Railway
Regional Border

N

Meteora monasteries

0   10 km
0   5 miles

Monasteries in the sky

Meteora

The cliff-top monasteries of the Meteora are among the strangest places in Greece. Vast, bulbous plugs of volcanic rock line a valley in the hills, which rise from the plains of Thessaly, near the small town of Kalambaka, and each pinnacle is crowned by an ancient Orthodox monastery or convent. Many of them are closed and deserted, but some are still in use and can be visited. Inside, monks' and nuns' cells surround old stone courtyards, and the walls and ceilings of the ancient churches and chapels are covered with sooty frescoes. A well-surfaced road now winds through the valley, but getting to most of the monasteries involves hiking up numerous steep steps. To avoid the crowds, steer clear of visiting at Easter or in mid-August.
ⓐ 150 km (95 miles) west of Volos; driving time two hours

Agias Triadas

Agias Triadas (Holy Trinity) is the least accessible monastery of the Meteora holy places, and getting here involves an arduous trek up multiple steep flights of stairs. If you are energetic and fit enough, it's worth making the ascent for the magnificent view of the whole valley.
ⓣ 24320 22220 ⓦ www.meteora-greece.com ⓛ 09.00–17.00 Fri–Wed (Apr–Oct); 10.00–15.00 Fri–Wed (Nov–Mar)

Agiou Nikolaou Anapafsas

Dedicated to St Nicholas, this little monastery church was built in the early 16th century and stands some distance from the others. ⓣ 24320 22375 ⓦ www.meteora-greece.com ⓛ 09.00–15.30 Sat–Thur (Apr–Oct)

Agiou Stefanou

Founded in 1545, this is the most accessible of the monasteries. It is also a good place to buy religious mementos representing Meteora in general. ⓣ 24320 22279 ⓦ www.meteora-greece.com ⓛ 09.00–13.30, 15.30–17.30 Tues–Sun (Apr–Oct); 09.30–13.00, 15.00–17.00 Tues–Sun (Nov–Mar)

Megalo Meteoron

Built in the mid-14th century, this is the oldest and largest monastery and contains a small museum dedicated to the history of the Meteora. ☎ 24320 22278 🌐 www.meteora-greece.com 🕐 09.00–17.00 Wed–Mon (Apr–Oct); 09.00–16.00 Thur–Mon (Nov–Mar)

Roussanou

The convent of Roussanou, dedicated to St Barbara (Agia Varvara), has the most breathtaking location of all the Meteora monasteries, and is set atop the highest of the valley's rock pinnacles. It also has some striking and gruesome mural paintings within its church of the Metamorphosis. These were painted in the mid-16th century. ☎ 24320 22649 🌐 www.meteora-greece.com 🕐 09.00–18.00 Thur–Tues (Apr–Oct); 09.00–16.00 Thur–Tues (Nov–Mar)

Varlaam

Dating from 1541, Varlaam is the second largest of the monasteries. Its refectory (the monks' dining room) is now a museum with exhibits that reflect the glory days of the Meteora monasteries. ☎ 24320 22277 🌐 www.meteora-greece.com 🕐 09.00–16.00 Wed–Mon (Apr–Oct); 09.00–16.00 Thur–Mon (Nov–Mar)

TAKING A BREAK

Taverna Arsenis £ Family-run taverna and guesthouse right at the foot of the Meteora, serving traditional Greek food and offering accommodation in modern en-suite bedrooms. ⓐ East road, Meteora, near Kalampaka ☎ 24320 24150 🌐 www.arsenis-meteora.gr 🕐 11.00–15.00, 18.00–23.00 daily

Meteoron Panorama ££ This affordable taverna serves oven-cooked Greek dishes and grilled meat and, as its name implies, has a wonderful view of the Meteora valley from its veranda. ⓐ Patriarchon Dimitriou 54, Kastraki ☎ 24320 78128 🕐 12.00–15.00, 19.00–23.00 daily

● *The spectacular location of the convent of Roussanou*

The beach at Damouhari; one of the film locations for Mamma Mia!

Home of the centaurs

The Pilion peninsula

The Pilion peninsula is one of the most beautiful places in Greece, and lies tantalisingly close to Skiathos – so close, in fact, that you could almost swim there. The Pilion is shaped like a cowboy's boot, with its curly toe enclosing a wide, calm bay, the Kolpos Pagassitikos (Pagasitic Gulf). Its highest point, Mount Pilion, rises 1,018 m (3,340 ft) above sea level – high enough to be snow-covered in winter, when it becomes one of Greece's few ski areas. In the myths of ancient Greece, the lush forests of the Pilion were the home of the half-human, half-equine centaurs. Plane and chestnut trees cover the peninsula's northern slopes, which are watered by many small streams even in high summer when the rest of Greece is parched dry, and the Pilion is famed for its apple orchards. The villages of the Pilion are among the most beautiful in Greece, with tall two- and three-storey mansions with grey-stone roofs and overhanging, half-timbered upper floors surrounding stone-paved squares shaded by huge plane trees.

Volos, at the head of the Kolpos Pagassitikos, is the gateway to the Pilion and other points on the mainland for travellers from the Sporades, with hydrofoil, fast catamaran and car-ferry connections to Skiathos, Skopelos and Alonnisos several times daily in summer. The journey time from Skiathos Town is around 45 minutes by hydrofoil. The easiest way to explore the Pilion is with a rented car from Volos; car rental can be arranged in advance through agencies in Skiathos Town, Skopelos Town and Patitiri on Alonnisos, or booked online with companies such as Hertz, Avis and Europcar, all of which have offices within walking distance of the Volos ferry harbour.

THINGS TO SEE & DO

Damouhari

This tiny bay with its rocky islets and headlands, crystal-clear water and white pebbles enjoyed a brief spell in the limelight when it was used as

a location for the film of the Abba musical *Mamma Mia!* in 2007. There are several amiable tavernas beside the miniature fishing harbour next to the beach, where you can still see the remains of an ancient Roman harbour just beneath the surface.

Makrinitsa

Makrinitsa is the closest to Volos of the Pilion's 'balcony villages', so called because their rather grand mansions are built around and above flagstoned village squares that look out over the hillside below and across the Pagasitic Gulf. Makrinitsa is well worth the short trip from Volos just for the view, but it also has a choice of charming small guesthouses in traditional homes and shady tavernas beneath enormous plane trees on its balcony square.

Milies

Well-off Greeks and some foreigners are buying and renovating derelict old houses on the outskirts of both Vizitsa and neighbouring Milies, and as a result the two villages are gradually merging. Like Makrinitsa, Milies has a spectacular balcony square and also has an interesting small folk museum dedicated to the old ways of the Pilion and its villages.

Pilion (Pelion) Railway

The narrow-gauge (600-mm/2-ft) Pilion Railway, built between 1892 and 1903, originally wound its way from Volos to the picturesque village of Milies, in the heart of the Pilion apple-growing country. It ceased commercial operation in 1971, but at weekends its miniature steam locomotives still pull carriages over the spectacular scenic route between Lehonia, on the coast near Volos, and Milies. There are several stone and one iron bridge on this mountainous section, and the train also negotiates two tunnels. Contact the Volos Tourist Information centre for timetables.

Volos Info ⓐ Corner of Lambraki and Sekeri, Volos ⓣ 24210 30940 ⓦ www.volos.gr ⓛ 09.00–12.00, 17.00–21.00 daily

⬥ *View from a walking trail near Tsangaradha*

Platanias

Midway along the southern coast, this is the best sandy beach on the Pilion. Almost 80 km (50 miles) from Volos by road, it is more easily reached by sea, and excursion boats shuttle across the narrow channel between here and Skiathos daily in summer.

Tsangaradha

Tsangaradha is the prettiest of the villages on the Pilion's lushly spectacular east coast, where thick, vividly green forests tumble down to white-pebble beaches and a dazzlingly clear turquoise sea. The village is spread over a wide area of wooded hillside, with tavernas and cafés on small squares connected by cobbled paths.

Vizitsa

Vizitsa is the most picturesque of the traditional villages on the west side of the Pilion peninsula. Set among thick woods and apple orchards, its whitewashed, half-timbered houses cluster around two tranquil squares surrounded by small cafés, and little streams run through the centre of the village.

Mount Olympus & Dion

Home of the gods

Mount Olympus, the legendary home of the Greek pantheon, looms over the Aegean coast, some 160 km (100 miles) north of Volos. Designated as a national park, it's a spectacular wilderness, where chamois roam and vultures and eagles soar. The views, even from the lower levels, can be breathtaking – as can the ascent to the top. More than 1,400 species of shrub, herb and wild flower can be found on the mountain, and the park shelters numerous rare birds, butterflies and reptiles.

Olympus is accessible to any reasonably fit adult – the only key requirement is a good pair of boots. From its slopes, the main coast road and the railway line to Volos and Thessaloniki look almost close enough to touch, and on a clear day you can look southeast to see Skiathos, Skopelos and Alonnisos off in the hazy blue distance.

You need two days and two nights to climb all the way to the summit of Olympus and return; if you only have one day, you can hike to the bunkhouse taverna at the 2,000-m (6,560-ft) level and back in six to eight hours, allowing time for lunch or a picnic.

Start from the car park about 5 km (3 miles) west of Litochoro village, around 1,000 m (3,300 ft) above sea level. From here, the steep zigzag hike through pine-wooded canyons to the alpine refuge at around the 2,000-m (6,560-ft) level takes three to four hours. Stay overnight at the refuge, which has a bunk-bedded dormitory and its own taverna, then allow six to eight hours to trek to the summit and back the following day. Stay a second night at the refuge, and descend the following morning.

Surprisingly, there is no record of anyone reaching the top of Mitikas, the highest peak of Mount Olympus, until the 20th century. The first climbers reached the summit in 1913. Olympus is frequently cloud-capped, and from the ancient temple-city of Dion, on the plains below the mountain, it is easy to see why the Greeks thought of it as the home of their gods. Although Dion dates from as early as the 5th century BC, most of the ruins here – including the remains of heated baths,

83

⬥ View of Mount Olympus, home of the ancient Greek gods

TIPS

- Except for the final traverse to the 2,917-m (9,571-ft) summit of Mitikas, across a short but knife-edged ridge, no technical skills or equipment are needed in summer.
- You'll need a small day-pack, good hillwalking footwear, sunblock, a hat, and for the walk to the summit you should allow at least two litres of water per person.
- The walk should not be attempted alone, and only skilled and well-equipped mountaineers should consider it between October and May.
- Litochoro is around two hours by bus or train from Volos. Take a taxi from the railway station (on the coast, 8 km/5 miles from Litochoro village) to the car park at the foot of Olympus and arrange for one to pick you up after your descent.

Alpine Travel operates escorted walks on Olympus and many other Greek mountain areas. ☎ 28210 50939 Ⓦ www.alpine.gr

Dion Archaeological Site 8km (5 miles) west of the main E75/N1 motorway ☎ 23510 53206 Ⓦ www.culture.gr ◷ 12.00–19.00 Mon, 08.00–19.30 Tues–Sat (Apr–Oct); 08.30–15.00 Tues–Sun (Nov–Mar) ❶ Admission charge

Greek Alpine Club ⓐ Ioannou Olympou 2, Litochoro ☎ 23520 84544 Ⓦ www.litohoro.gr

a theatre, some excellent mosaics and a Christian basilica – date from the later Roman era. The ponds and channels around the site are home to families of coypus – the descendants of escapees from the fur farms of Kastoria. The small, modern museum in the village has an interesting collection of finds from the sanctuary at Dion dedicated to the Roman-Egyptian goddess Isis.

Thessaloniki

You can visit Greece's exciting 'second city' by high-speed hydrofoil ferry, or by air from Skiathos, and it's well worth making the journey. Thessaloniki is a lively, youthful city, home to one of Greece's largest universities, and has some of the country's best restaurants, exciting nightlife in the buzzing **Ladadika** area, and an array of world-class heritage sites. Relics of the Roman, Byzantine and Ottoman empires are scattered around its busy streets, and its huge market area is an attraction in its own right.

The golden treasures of Macedonian kings are on display in the city's archaeological museum, and Thessaloniki also has a collection of fascinating specialist museums. The city is built around a vast, almost landlocked, bay, the Thermaic Gulf, and its streets rise in tiers towards a hilltop crowned with the ruined walls of an ancient fortress, Eptapyrgio. Thessaloniki's main thoroughfare, Egnatia Odos, follows the line of an ancient Roman highway, the Via Egnatia, and its waterfront esplanade, Leoforos Nikis, is lined with shops and smart cafés. Midway along Nikis, Plateia Aristotelous (Aristotle Square) is surrounded by café terraces and is the social hub of the city.

The **Thessaloniki Office of Tourism Directorate** (ⓐ Tsimiski 136 ⓣ 2310 21100 ⓔ rour-the@otenet.gr ⓛ 08.00–20.00 Mon–Fri, 08.00–14.00 Sat) has friendly, English-speaking staff.

Most of the city's main attractions are within easy walking distance of each other. The best days to visit are Tuesday to Saturday, as several

GETTING TO THESSALONIKI

Argo Airways, based in Volos, flies seaplane services to Thessaloniki from Skiathos, Skopelos and Alonnisos via Volos.
ⓐ Argonavton 16, Volos ⓣ 24210 23007 ⓦ www.argoairways.com
Planet Seaways operates day trips by hydrofoil from Skiathos and Skopelos to Thessaloniki in summer. ⓐ Tsimiski 34, Thessaloniki
ⓣ 23102 63030

museums are closed or have shorter opening hours on Mondays, and the market area is mostly closed on Sundays.

THINGS TO SEE & DO

Ancient Forum

The Ancient Forum was the heart of Thessaloniki in its 4th-century Roman heyday, when it would have been alive with shops, public affairs and services. It is still being excavated and rediscovered, and until the work is complete the remains of its open-air theatre and rows of columns can only be viewed from outside, but it is well worth the short walk from Plateia Aristotelous. ⓐ Plateia Arheas Agoras Ⓦ www.culture.gr Ⓛ Can be viewed from any side of the square 24 hours

Arch of Galerius

Built by the Roman Emperor Galerius in AD 303 to mark his victory over the Persians, this triumphal arch is carved with depictions of battle and Galerius' vanquished enemies. ⓐ East end of Egnatia Odos Ⓛ 24 hours

Byzantine churches

More than a dozen historic Byzantine churches, some of them dating back to the early centuries of the Christian era, stand amid the modern buildings of Thessaloniki. Several are listed as UNESCO World Heritage Sites.

Among the most impressive and easiest to visit, as they are located close to the city centre, are the great church of **Agia Sofia** (Holy Wisdom), built in the 8th century AD, and the huge church of **Agios Dimitrios** (Greece's largest church), which was built in the 8th century and completely rebuilt after being destroyed in the great fire that swept through the city in 1917. ⓐ Agia Sofia, Plateia Agia Sofias; and Agios Dimitrios, Plateia Agiou Dimitriou Ⓦ www.culture.gr Ⓛ 09.00–13.00 Tues–Sun, closed Mon

🔺 *Aristotle Square, Thessaloniki*

Eptapyrgio

To discover **Ano Poli** ('the high city'), the oldest and most picturesque part of Thessaloniki, hike uphill from the Rotunda (see page 90) following the line of the old Byzantine ramparts. From the observation areas at the top, you can see the hilltop fortress known as the Eptapyrgio ('seven-towered'). This formidable stronghold dominated the city for almost 1,000 years, and was still used as a prison until 1989. Restoration continues, and above its huge inner gateway can be seen typically Byzantine reliefs of mythical birds and beasts and Ottoman-carved Koranic inscriptions. There are fantastic views from this hilltop fortress.

Markets

Thessaloniki's market area sprawls across several blocks of the city centre. It's a colourful spectacle, with dozens of stalls piled high with brightly coloured flowers, fruit and vegetables, tubs and sacks of herbs, spices and olives, and weird-looking seafood on beds of crushed ice. Old-style tavernas around the market area serve great Greek food at bargain prices. The oldest market hall is the **Bezesteni**, close to the corner of Solomou and Venizelou, built in 1459 and instantly recognisable with its six-domed roof. The **Vlali** area is the city's main produce market, and a great place to shop for picnic materials or for Greek produce such as olives (at least 40 different kinds are on sale), herbs and handicrafts such as carved wooden utensils and bowls, and hand-woven baskets. The **Modiano** market, housed in a neoclassical hall built in 1922, has some of the city's best delicatessens and traditional tavernas.

All three markets open early (around 08.00) and are open every day except Sunday and public holidays. They are at their best first thing, with most shops and stalls closing by 17.00 at the latest.

Museum of Byzantine Culture

This museum is another must-see. Glowing gold and crimson icons from the heyday of the Byzantine Empire are the jewels in the crown of this museum's dazzling collection. ⓐ Stratou 2 ❶ 23108 68570 Ⓦ www.mbp.gr ❻ 12.30–19.00 Mon, 08.00–19.00 Tues–Sun (Apr–Oct);

10.30–17.00 Mon, 08.00–17.00 Tues–Fri, 08.00–14.30 Sat & Sun
(Nov–Mar) ❶ Admission charge

Rotunda

This massive circular brick building with its tiled domes has undergone
many changes since it was built in AD 306 as a mausoleum for the
Emperor Galerius, though he was never actually buried there. A century
after his death it was turned into a Christian church dedicated to Agios
Georgios (St George), and after the Ottoman conquest of Greece it
became a mosque. The slim minaret that stands beside it is the only one
left in Thessaloniki, a city which, until the early 20th century, had many
of these Muslim prayer towers. Inside, some of its splendid medieval
mosaics have been preserved and restoration continues. ⓐ Plateia Agios
Georgiou ❶ 23102 45309 ⓦ www.culture.gr ❶ 09.00–13.00 Tues–Sun,
closed Mon

Thessaloniki Archaeological Museum

The highlight of this must-see museum in Thessaloniki is the
golden treasure from the tombs of Alexander's ancestors at Pella
and Vergina. ⓐ Manolis Andronikou 6 ❶ 23108 30538
ⓦ www.macedonian-heritage.gr ❶ 14.00–20.30 Mon, 08.00–20.30
Tues–Sun ❶ Admission charge

White Tower

The best-known symbol of Thessaloniki is more than 500 years old and
once formed part of the city's defences. It was also a prison and a place
of execution, nicknamed the 'Bloody Tower'. ⓐ East end of Leoforos Nikis
❶ 23102 67832 ⓦ www.mbp.gr ❶ 08.30–15.00 Tues–Sun, closed Mon
❶ Admission charge

TAKING A BREAK

Ouzou Melathron £ You can't miss this huge *ouzeri* close to the corner of
Tsimiskis and El Venizelou – its façade is covered with larger-than-life

🔺 *The 15th-century White Tower*

figures of street performers, including musicians, a mighty weight-lifter and a dancing bear. The food is Greek-style *meze* and it's very popular with locals. ⓐ Karpi 21–34 ⓣ 23102 75016 ⓦ www.ouzoumelathron.gr ⓛ 12.00–01.00 daily

Bita ££ Spotless, stylish, light and airy surroundings (tables inside and out) with a marvellous menu that blends Greek ingredients in new ways. Perfect location for lunch while visiting the Museum of Byzantine Culture and the Archaeological Museum, which is just across the road. ⓐ 3 Septembriou 2 ⓣ 23108 69695 ⓛ 12.00–15.00, 19.00–24.00 Tues–Sat, 12.00–15.00 Sun & Mon

1900 ££ This large and well-known *ouzeri* is a good stop for a cold drink and a snack, a longer lunch, or an evening out in the older part of Thessaloniki. ⓐ Kleious 30, Tsinari ⓣ 23102 75462 ⓛ 12.00–16.00, 19.00–01.00 daily

Zithos ££ This brasserie-style restaurant-bar in the heart of the Ladadika district, near the harbour, serves a wide choice of beers and traditional Greek snacks and dishes with a modern twist. ⓐ Katouni 5 ⓣ 23105 40284 ⓦ www.zithos.gr ⓛ 12.00–01.00 daily

Seafood £££ On the waterfront near the museums, the seafood restaurant of Thessaloniki's poshest hotel is stylish and – depending on what you order – can be surprisingly affordable, too. ⓐ Makedonia Palace Hotel, Alexandrou 2 ⓣ 23108 97197 ⓦ www.classicalhotels.com ⓛ 12.00–15.00, 19.00–23.00 daily

● *Welcome to Banana beach's cocktail bar*

LIFESTYLE
Island life

Food & drink

EATING HABITS

Greeks tend to breakfast lightly and dine late, and when going out to a restaurant few Greeks would consider sitting down to dinner any earlier than 21.00. Lunch can often be a leisurely affair. On Skiathos, the choice of places to eat is wide and cosmopolitan, ranging from traditional tavernas to fast-food joints, pizzerias and restaurants serving a variety of modern Mediterranean and international cuisine. On the other islands, the culinary emphasis is on traditional Greek cooking. Some of the best food can be discovered in little old-fashioned *ouzeries*, frequented mainly by locals, in village backstreets, but you will pay a premium to eat and drink at a harbour-side taverna that caters mainly to visitors – especially if those visitors happen to be wealthy Greek yacht-owners. That said, if a restaurant has a well-off Greek clientele it is much more likely to serve really good food.

Greek restaurants come with a variety of labels, which can be bewildering to the first-time visitor. There is little to choose between a traditional restaurant or *estiatorion* and a taverna, both of which serve a wide range of dishes. Restaurants specialising in grilled meat dishes – usually lamb, chicken and pork, grilled on the spit – are known as *psistaria*, while a seafood restaurant is known as a *psarotaverna*. In such restaurants, fish is usually priced by weight – you choose your fish, which is then weighed in front of you and priced accordingly. An *ouzeri* or *mezedopolion* serves Greece's national spirit – *ouzo* – by the glass or the bottle, wine or beer, with an array of snacks and small dishes. A *kafeneion* is a traditional café that serves Greek-style coffee, instant coffee and sometimes filter coffee, tea (usually served without milk, and in a glass), soft drinks and a limited range of alcoholic drinks, usually including *ouzo*, Greek-style brandy, wine and beer. A *zacharoplasteion* is a pastry shop which usually serves coffee and spirits as well as an assortment of sweet and creamy cakes and other desserts, and Greeks often move on after dinner to a *zacharoplasteion* for dessert. Greece's home-grown fast food is *giros* or *souvlaki*, grilled on the spit and served with vegetables, chips and yoghurt in pitta bread.

LICENSING HOURS, OPENING TIMES & SMOKING

All Greek eating places serve alcohol at all times; it's not unusual in an old-style café in a market district or beside a fishing harbour to see traders or fishermen who have been at work since before dawn enjoying a shot of *ouzo* with their morning coffee. A smoking ban in public places was introduced in 2002; however, restaurants are required to provide non-smoking tables, but few operate a blanket ban on smoking. Cafés in towns and cities usually open around 08.00 or earlier to cater to early-rising workers, and stay open until 24.00 or later. Cafés in resort areas open around 09.00 or 10.00. Most restaurants open between 12.00 and 15.00 for lunch, then close until at least 19.00 before reopening for dinner until around 24.00. In summer, many establishments stay open as late as 02.00. Most places are open seven days a week in summer, but virtually all eating places, hotels and guesthouses on Skiathos, Skopelos and Alonnisos close from the end of October until April or May.

LOCAL FOOD

The waters around Skiathos and the neighbouring islands provide a superb choice of seafood, from anchovies and sardines to tuna, grouper, red mullet and sea bream, prawns, mussels and other shellfish, lobster,

FETA FEUD

From being a purely Greek delicacy, feta gained worldwide popularity, with other countries such as Denmark, Germany, France and the Netherlands producing their own versions. For almost 20 years, Greece petitioned the EU to ban foreign farmers from designating their cheeses as feta, claiming the label should apply exclusively to cheeses made from the milk of Greek sheep or goats. A European Court of Justice ruling in Greece's favour came into effect at the end of 2007 – so any feta you buy, at least within the EU, should be the real thing.

squid and octopus. More unusual seafoods include sea urchins, which are found in huge numbers around Greece's coasts.

Meat is usually grilled, and lamb, chicken and pork are favoured. Typically Greek dishes served in traditional grill restaurants include roasted sheep's head, complete with eyeballs, or *kokoretsi*, a confection of sheep's liver, kidney and other offal bound together with intestines, then grilled on the spit. Greek cuisine also features a lot of oven-cooked dishes, which are simmered slowly in oil for hours. These include the ever-popular *moussaka*, made with minced lamb layered with aubergine and béchamel sauce. Other oven dishes include *giouvetsi* (meat baked in a clay pot with pasta), *kleftiko* (lamb sealed in foil and greaseproof paper and slow-roasted) and *stifado* (meat or seafood simmered in red wine and onions).

Greeks rarely drink alcohol unless it is accompanied by food, and a glass of *ouzo*, wine or beer usually comes with a complimentary saucer of sunflower seeds, olives, cubes of cheese or slices of sausage, known as *meze* or *poikilia*.

VEGETARIANS

Vegetarians who are happy to live on salad, fresh fruit and cheese for a while will find themselves well catered for in Greece, and the traditional Greek salad is a meal in its own right. To order it without cheese, ask for *angourodomatasalata*. There are also a number of vegetable dips, such as *tsatsiki*, made from garlic, yoghurt and cucumber, and *fava*, made from puréed beans. Cooked vegetable dishes include peppers or tomatoes stuffed with rice and herbs, broad beans in tomato sauce, vegetable stews such as *fasolakia* (made with green beans) and *papoutsakia* (baked and stuffed aubergine), as well as cheese or spinach pies made with filo pastry (*tyropita* and *spanikopita*).

DESSERTS & SWEETS

Visitors with a sweet tooth find themselves in heaven in Greece, where pastry shops serve a mouthwatering choice of sticky cream and chocolate cakes, and pastries flavoured with honey, nuts and spices such as *baklava*, *loukoumadhes*, *kataifi* and *bougatsa*.

DRINKS

Greek wine has improved enormously in recent years, with wineries all over the mainland producing red, white and rosé wines that bear comparison with the products of better-known winemaking countries such as France, Italy and Spain. Retsina, the resin-flavoured white wine of Greece, is cheap but is also an acquired taste – even Greeks sometimes mix it with lemonade or cola.

Another acquired taste is Greece's national spirit, *ouzo*, which is strongly flavoured with aniseed and turns cloudy when mixed with ice or water. *Tsipouro*, a grappa-like spirit, is usually drunk neat, in tiny glasses, after a meal. Greek brandy is on the sweet side but is a pleasant evening tipple. Several brands of lager-style beer are made in Greece, and a wide range of imported wines, beers and spirits is offered everywhere, as are all the well-known international soft drink brands.

Greek tap water is generally safe to drink, but is usually heavily chlorinated. Tap water on Alonnisos is brackish and tastes unpleasant. Mineral water is for sale everywhere.

● *Enjoy alfresco dining and drinking in beautiful settings*

Menu decoder

Here are some of the dishes you might encounter while visiting the area.

GENERAL

Bira Beer
Frappe Iced coffee
Gala Milk
Kafe (elliniko) Coffee (Greek)
Kafe (gallico) Coffee (filter)
Krasi Wine
Meli Honey
Nero (metalliko) Water (mineral)
Nes Instant coffee
Pagota Ice cream
Patates tiganites Chips
Psomi Bread
Tsai Tea
Tyri Cheese
Yiaourti Yoghurt

TYPICAL GREEK DISHES

Dolmades Vine leaves stuffed with rice, herbs and maybe meat
Fasolakia Stewed green beans
Gemista Stuffed tomatoes
Gigantes Stewed broad beans in tomato sauce
Giouvetsi Meat slow-cooked in a clay pot with pasta
Horiatiki Salad of onions, tomatoes, cucumber, pepper and feta cheese
Keftedhes Meatballs
Kleftiko Roast lamb
Kokoretsi Grilled offal
Kolokythakia tiganita Fried courgettes
Melitsanes tiganites Fried aubergines
Moussaka Minced lamb baked with aubergines in béchamel sauce
Paidakia Lamb chops
Papoutsakia Baked aubergine stuffed with onion and tomato
Pastitsio Macaroni pie
Psarosoupa Fish soup
Soutsoukakia Meat patties
Spanakopita Spinach pie
Stifado Pork stewed in red wine and onions
Tyropita Cheese pie

MENU ITEMS & COOKING TERMS

In all the resorts on Skiathos and the Sporades, restaurant menus are multilingual, although the translations from Greek into English can sometimes be eccentric (it is not unusual for a menu to feature 'fried squits' (squid), 'lamp shops' (lamb chops) or even 'smashed bowels in roasted spit' (kokoretsi)).

Ahini Sea urchin
Alati Salt
Angouro Cucumber
Arni Lamb
Astakos Langouste (spiny lobster)
Avga Eggs
Barbounia Red mullet
Domata Tomato
Elies Olives
Garidhes Prawns
Glyka Sweets
Heirino Pork
Horta Boiled greens
Hymo Juice
Kalamares Squid

Kapnisto Smoked
Karpousi Watermelon
Katsiki Goat
Kotopoulo Chicken
Lahanika Vegetables
Lavraki Sea bass
Maridhes Whitebait
Mayeirefta Oven cooked
Mydhia Mussels
Oktapodhi Octopus
Piponi Honeydew melon
Psari Fish
Scharas Grilled
Thalassina Seafood
Tiganita Fried
Tsipoura Gilthead bream

Shopping

On all three islands, mini-markets in the main villages and in resorts provide all your basic holiday needs, such as sunblock, bottled water and nappies, and there are plenty of gift shops selling swimwear, children's clothes and beach accessories.

There are a good range of shops in **Skiathos Town**. All essentials can be found there; it has several pharmacies and supermarkets. The main shopping street is Papadiamantis, which has numerous shops selling beach toys, leisure wear, cheap fashion accessories and fairly predictable souvenirs – none of which are made locally and few of which are even made in Greece. However, a few attractive shops in Skiathos Town stand out from the crowd:

Aquarius 'L' Very attractive and imaginative handmade silver, ceramics and wooden toys. ⓐ Corner of Papadiamantis and Panora ⓣ 24270 21912 ⓦ www.aquarius-l.gr/index.php ⓛ 10.00–20.00 daily

Mikrokosmos Handcrafted, collectable baubles, bangles and beads. ⓐ Nikotsara 30, Skiathos Town ⓣ 24270 24537 ⓛ 10.00–13.00, 17.00–20.00 daily

Odysseus Expensive gold, silver and diamonds, but also small and more affordable bracelet charms, rings and pendants. ⓐ Papadiamantis 15 ⓣ 24270 53790 ⓛ 10.00–22.00 daily

Workshop Jewellery Original handcrafted contemporary gold and silver. ⓐ Epifaniadou 2 and Syngrou ⓣ 24270 24484 ⓦ www.skiathos workshop.gr ⓛ 09.00–12.00, 17.00–22.00 daily

On **Alonnisos**, everyday needs can be found in Patitiri, which has two pharmacies, several English-language bookshops and supermarkets, as well as numerous shops selling swimwear and beach toys. Palaio Chorio is full of small craft shops and galleries. Try the following:

Alonissiotissa Traditional sweets, savouries and preserves from Alonnisos, such as flavoured honey, home-made marzipan, pasta and cheeses. ⓐ Pelasgon, Patitiri ⓣ 24240 66373 ⓛ 11.00–20.00 daily

Gallery 5 Danish expat Bente Keller and her Greek husband, Elias

Tsoukanas, sell pretty watercolour paintings, prints, cards, handmade candles and their definitive guide to walking in Alonnisos. ⓐ Palaio Chorio ⓣ 24240 65931 ⓦ www.bentekeller.gr ⓛ 11.00–21.00 daily

Gefsi Physis Herbs, honey, flavoured olive oil and olive oil products, sponges and many more traditional tastes and products. ⓐ Palaio Chorio ⓣ 24240 65593

Gorgona Sells replica and original *komboloi* (the traditional worry beads older Greek men still habitually carry), antiques, woven wool bags and rugs, and a range of other crafts. ⓐ Palaio Chorio ⓣ 24240 66108

Xeironax Handmade silver, textiles, puppets and other traditional wooden toys. ⓐ Palaio Chorio ⓣ 24240 66287

On **Skopelos**, everyday needs are catered for in Skopelos Town, which also has a range of small art galleries and craft shops, such as:

Gray Gallery This welcoming little shop displays and sells nice paintings by artists local and foreign alike. ⓐ Skopelos Town ⓣ 24240 24266 ⓛ 09.00–20.00 daily

Ploumisti Art Gallery Colourful ceramics in the typical Skopelos style, woodcarvings and textiles. ⓐ Skopelos Town ⓣ 24240 22059 ⓦ www.skopelosgallery.com ⓛ 10.00–13.00, 17.00–22.00 daily

Potoki Gold and silver, copies of Byzantine icons, ceramics and prints. ⓐ New Marina, Skopelos Town ⓣ 24240 22929 ⓦ www.potokijewel.gr

◖ *Handmade candles from Gallery 5, Alonnisos*

Children

BEACHES

Skiathos, with its big beaches of soft yellow sand, is one of the most child-friendly resort islands in Greece. Most beaches throughout the Sporades are clean and reasonably safe for children, but few beaches have lifeguards on duty. Hazards include black and spiny sea urchins on rocky shores.

CHILD-MINDING

Child-minding and babysitting facilities are not widely available in hotels on Skiathos and the Sporades. If you require such facilities, your best option is to book your holiday through a major tour operator, which may be able to offer childminders and babysitters as part of the accommodation package.

RESTAURANTS

Children are welcome in all restaurants in the Sporades, but few places have special facilities for children, or children's menus. Adventurous children may be fascinated by the Greek habit of cooking and serving fish dishes complete with head, tail and bones. For the less adventurous eaters, there are plenty of places serving pizzas, pasta and burgers.

SPORTS & ACTIVITIES

Almost all the resorts on Skiathos have a choice of watersports for older children, including pedalos and canoes. However, lifejackets and supervision are not always provided and children should always be accompanied by an adult. Scuba-diving lessons for children aged ten and over are available on Skiathos, and dinghy-sailing lessons are available for children in Skopelos Town.

Dolphin Diving Center offers sample dives and qualification courses for beginners as well as a range of dives for experienced divers (see page 39).

Skiathos Riding Center at Koukounaries has two gentle donkeys for younger children, and horses for adults and older children (see page 30).

WILDLIFE

Children with an interest in wildlife will enjoy the butterflies, colourful wild flowers and kingfishers around the amazing lagoon at Koukounaries on Skiathos. Small streams flow from the hills down to several of the south-coast beaches on Skiathos, forming lush, small, reed-lined lagoons behind the sand. Children can spot frogs, fire-bellied toads, tadpoles, small fish and vivid red-and-blue dragonflies in and around these tiny oases.

Children enjoy donkey rides; the donkeys appreciate fly fringes

Sports & activities

Skiathos and the neighbouring islands offer plenty of options for those seeking an active holiday. Watersports are in abundance, as you would expect, with waterskiing, wakeboarding, windsurfing and a variety of inflatable rides available at virtually every beach. Larger resort beaches offer the widest range of powered watersports. Beneath the waves, scuba diving is increasingly popular, and the very clear and calm waters around the Sporades make this an excellent place to try diving for the first time. On land, the gentle, wooded hills and networks of old mule paths make all three islands – but especially Alonnisos and Skopelos – attractive places for walkers.

RIDING
Skiathos Riding Center at Koukounaries has a troop of Yugoslav-Arab horses and two gentle donkeys for younger children. ⓐ Bus stop 25, Koukounaries ⓣ 24270 49750 ⓦ www.skiathos-horse-riding.gr ⓛ 09.00–12.00, 15.00–18.00 daily

SCUBA DIVING
There are scuba-diving outfits on all three islands, offering a range of dives, including trial dives for first-time divers, qualifying courses, and wreck and reef dives for experienced divers.
Dolphin Diving Center ⓐ Nostos Village Holiday Resort, Tzaneria, Skiathos ⓣ 24270 21599 ⓛ 09.00–19.00 daily
Ikion Sport ⓐ Steni Vala harbour, Alonnisos ⓣ 24240 65158 ⓦ www.ikiongroup.gr
Poseidonas Diving Centre ⓐ Patitiri harbour, Alonnisos ⓣ 24240 66100

TENNIS
The tennis court at the **Nostos Village Holiday Resort** on Skiathos, immediately inland from Tzaneria beach, can be rented by the hour by non-residents. ⓐ Bus stop 12, Tzaneria, Skiathos ⓦ www.nostosvillage.gr ⓛ 10.00–18.00 daily

Watersports opportunities on Big Banana beach

WALKING

On Skopelos, British expat **Heather Parsons** leads guided walks around Skopelos Town and the surrounding countryside (see page 51). Walking tours of Alonnisos and the marine park islands are provided by **Albedo Travel**, and there are also herbal tours, to track down healing plants, led by Waltrand Helma Alberti. Alternatively, walkers can buy *Alonnisos on Foot* and make their own way over the island (see page 63 for details).

WATERSPORTS

There are watersports centres renting equipment for powered and unpowered watersports at all the main resorts on Skiathos, Skopelos and Alonnisos. Pedalos, kayaks, catamarans, windsurfers, jet-skis and waterskis are available. The renting companies change from year to year so are not listed here, but no reservations are necessary – just turn up and go.

YOGA

On Alonnisos, classes for beginners and experienced Hatha yoga and Ashtanga yoga practitioners are offered in Palaio Chorio and at several hotels around the island by **Kalithea Yoga** (see page 64).

Festivals & events

MARCH/APRIL
Easter
The Greek Orthodox Easter is a movable feast with dates that can be up to three weeks earlier or later than the Western Easter. It is Greece's most important religious festival, with processions to village churches and elaborate church services. Easter reaches a crescendo at midnight on Easter Saturday with fireworks and candlelit processions, followed by family feasting and dancing on Easter Sunday.

Agios Georgios (23 April)
Agios Georgios (St George) is the patron saint of flocks and shepherds and is revered all over Greece. His feast is celebrated with special enthusiasm on Skyros (see page 8).

MAY
Protomagia (May Day/Labour Day) (1 May)
May Day is a typically Greek mix of pagan and Christian tradition and modern politics, when families pick wild poppies and other flowers to weave into garlic wreaths that are hung above doorways to fend off evil spirits. Meanwhile, left-wing parties and trade unions rally in cities and major towns to keep the red flag flying.

JULY
Agia Paraskevi (26 July)
This saint's day is celebrated at the church named after her on Skiathos with music and dancing, when many women wear their traditional island costumes.

Athens Festival (throughout July)
Highbrow season of classical and orchestral music, drama and dance, as well as fringe events at venues ancient and modern throughout Athens.

Skopelos International Guitar Festival (last week in July)
Performances and master-classes by maestros of acoustic and classical guitar from all over the world.

AUGUST
Koimisis tis Theotokou (Assumption of the Virgin) (15 August)
Millions of Greeks from the cities and from overseas return to their ancestral villages for Koimisis, the biggest family event in the Greek calendar.

DATES FOR YOUR DIARY!
Easter, Protomagia and Koimisis can present challenges for anyone planning to travel within Greece around these dates. Many bars and restaurants close or open only limited hours over Easter, and workers' organisations often choose Protomagia for strikes and demonstrations, which can bring cities such as Thessaloniki and Athens grinding to a halt. With millions of people on the move, train, plane, bus and ferry tickets are hard to find around Koimisis. Accommodation, too, is at a premium around Easter and Koimisis, and anyone planning to travel within Greece around this time needs to make arrangements well in advance.

---

❿ Fast hydrofoils connect the islands of Skiathos, Skopelos and Alonnisos

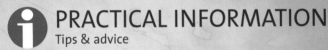

PRACTICAL INFORMATION
Tips & advice

Accommodation

All hotels and guesthouses on Skiathos and the Sporades close from late October until the Greek Easter. Some do not reopen until May. There are a few luxury hotels on Skiathos, but if you're looking for a villa holiday it is best to book through a package tour operator. On Skopelos and Alonnisos, accommodation tends to be in smaller hotels and guesthouses. The price guide below is based on the average price for a double room with bed and breakfast:

£ under €80   ££ €80–€150   £££ more than €150

ALONNISOS

Konstantina Studios £ Ten self-catering studios and apartments sleeping two to four people. No pool, but a pretty garden with hammocks under the trees. ⓐ Palio Chorio (3 km/2 miles) from Patitiri, Alonnisos ⓣ 24240 66165 ⓦ www.konstantinastudios.gr ⓛ Closed Nov–Easter

Milia Village ££ This friendly, family-run hotel is simply the best place to stay on Alonnisos, with a seawater pool and amazing views. The beach at Milia is a five-minute walk and Patitiri's bars and restaurants are a five-minute taxi ride. ⓐ Milia, Alonnisos ⓣ 24240 66032 ⓦ www.milia-bay.gr

Marpunta Village Hotel £££ Club-style resort hotel with wide range of facilities including two beaches, pool, tennis courts, disco, cinema, open-air theatre and choice of bars and restaurants. ⓐ Marpounta, 2 km (1 mile) south of Patitiri, Alonnisos ⓣ 24240 65212 ⓦ www.santikos hotels.com ⓛ Closed Nov–Easter

SKIATHOS

Hotel Mato £ Small (just eight rooms), affordable and friendly hotel in the old part of town. Rooms are large, comfortable and well designed. ⓐ 25 Martiou 30, Panagia Limni, Skiathos Town ⓣ 24270 22186 ⓦ www.matoskiathos.com ⓛ Closed late Oct–Easter

Plaza Hotel ££ Only 100 m (110 yds) above Kanapitsa beach, the Plaza is a modern, low-rise three-star resort hotel with a large pool and good facilities for families. ⓐ Platanias, Skiathos ❶ 24270 21971 Ⓦ www.greekhotel.com/sporades/skiathos/kanapitsa/plaza ⓛ Closed late Oct–Easter

Skiathos Princess Hotel £££ By far the finest family resort hotel in the Sporades – and one of the best in Greece – the Skiathos Princess is set in lush gardens overlooking a vividly blue bay. It has a large pool, semi-private beach, a 'wellness centre' and a wide range of activities. ⓐ 7 km (4 miles) from Skiathos Town ❶ 24270 49731 Ⓦ www.skiathos princess.com ⓛ Closed Oct–May

SKOPELOS
Hotel Dionysos £ This low-rise hotel on a hill above Skopelos Town offers considerable luxury at an affordable price and has fabulous views. There's a pool, pool bar and restaurant, a garden full of flowers and palm trees, and rooms have English-language satellite TV and minibar. ⓐ Limani Skopelou ❶ 24240 23210 Ⓦ www.dionyssoshotel.com ⓛ Closed Nov–Mar

Prince Stafilos ££ This is one of the best-value options on Skopelos, with a peaceful location, an excellent restaurant, a full range of in-room facilities and 24-hour service. ⓐ Livadhi, Skopelos ❶ 24240 22775 Ⓦ www.prince-stafilos.gr ⓛ Closed Nov–Mar

THESSALONIKI
Makedonia Palace £££ The magnificent and luxurious Makedonia Palace, Thessaloniki's largest and grandest city hotel, stands on the waterfront, with fabulous views of the Thermaic Gulf. It has several excellent restaurants and immaculate service. ⓐ M Alexandrou 2, Thessaloniki ❶ 23108 97197 Ⓦ www.classicalhotels.com

Preparing to go

GETTING THERE

The only practical way to get to the Sporades from the UK is by air, and the most convenient way is to take a charter flight direct to Skiathos with one of the airlines owned by a big holiday company, such as **Thomas Cook Airlines** (ⓦ www.thomascookairlines.co.uk) or **Thomsonfly** (ⓦ flights.thomson.co.uk). These offer package holidays that include accommodation, transfers to and from airports, and car hire. Booking a package holiday through a tour operator does not have to be more expensive than making your own arrangements, and in the Sporades it is usually cheaper than doing it yourself, and is certainly less time consuming.

You can also get to the Sporades via Athens. Greece's first airline, **Olympic Air** (ⓣ 0870 606 0460 ⓦ www.olympicair.com), flies to Athens from the UK and operates local flights to Skiathos. Other airlines flying to Athens from the UK include:

Aegean Airlines, the independent Greek airline ⓣ 00 30 21062 61000 ⓦ www.aegeanair.com

British Airways ⓣ 0844 493 0787 ⓦ www.ba.com

easyJet ⓣ 0870 000 0000 ⓦ www.easyjet.com

Many people are aware that air travel emits CO_2, which contributes to climate change. You may be interested in the possibility of lessening the environmental impact of your flight through the charity **Climate Care**, which offsets your CO_2 by funding environmental projects around the world. Visit ⓦ www.jpmorganclimatecare.com for more information.

Seaplane company **Argo Airways** (ⓣ 24210 23007 ⓦ www.argo airways.com), based in Volos, flies short hops to all of the Sporades as well as to Athens and Thessaloniki, and fares are surprisingly cheap.

Frequent ferries and hydrofoils operate from the mainland port of Volos to Skiathos and also connect Skiathos with Skopelos and Alonnisos. Journey time is around 45 minutes to Skopelos and between 90 minutes and 2 hours to Alonnisos.

TOURISM INFORMATION

In the UK, the Greek National Tourist Office (GNTO) (ⓐ 4 Conduit Street, London W1S 2DJ ⓣ 020 7495 9300 ⓦ www.gnto.co.uk) can provide general information about Greece.

BEFORE YOU LEAVE

There are no compulsory immunisation requirements. If you require a prescription medicine, bring an adequate supply with you as not all the villages in the Sporades have fully stocked pharmacies. Similarly, sunblock and suntan lotions are not available everywhere, so bring plenty with you. A basic medical kit should also include mosquito repellent, antihistamine tablets for stings and bites, and a diarrhoea remedy.

❶ Note that painkillers containing even a small amount of codeine, which are available without prescription in the UK, are classified as illegal drugs in Greece.

ENTRY FORMALITIES

UK and Irish nationals require only a passport to enter Greece and may stay as long as they wish. Citizens of EU countries within the Schengen Agreement zone need only a national identity card. Citizens of the USA, Canada, Australia, New Zealand and South Africa do not require a visa for a stay of up to 90 days.

Normal EU customs rules apply. Non-EU visitors may bring in 200 cigarettes, 50 cigars or 250 g of tobacco, 1 litre of spirits, 2 litres of wine or liqueurs, 50 ml of perfume and 250 ml of eau de toilette.

MONEY

The euro is the currency in Greece and is available in 1, 5, 10, 20, 50, 100, 200 and 500 euro notes. In practice, most places do not accept notes in denominations of more than 100 euros. Coin denominations are: 1 cent, 2 cents, 5 cents, 10 cents, 20 cents, 50 cents, 1 euro and 2 euros.

Some foreign currency can be exchanged at banks and in hotels, but it is advisable either to carry cash in euros or to buy a cash passport pre-paid debit card preloaded with euros, or euro traveller's cheques. The

American Express website (Ⓦ www.americanexpress.com/usetc) gives detailed information about where traveller's cheques are accepted.

MasterCard and Visa are widely accepted in hotels, shops and restaurants, but most smaller establishments prefer payment in cash. American Express and Diners Club cards are accepted only in larger hotels, expensive shops in major cities, and by most airlines and car-rental agencies.

ATMs (which accept all major debit and credit cards using the Maestro and Cirrus systems) are available in the main villages on Skiathos, Skopelos, Alonnisos and in Volos. Customers can obtain information about their nearest ATM at Ⓦ www.thomascook.com/cashpassport

CLIMATE

The climate of the Sporades is marginally cooler all year round than that of the southern Aegean islands, with breezes that take some of the edge off the summer heat. Maximum temperatures peak at up to 35°C (95°F) in July, the hottest month. Winters are generally mild but wet, with temperatures rarely falling below 10°C (50°F).

BAGGAGE ALLOWANCE

Baggage allowances vary from airline to airline and there are no hard and fast rules on maximum weight for hand luggage and checked-in (hold) luggage nor for the number of pieces of luggage you may check in. Many airlines now charge extra for hold luggage. Generally, only one piece of carry-on luggage per passenger is permitted. Baggage allowances can usually be found on the 'frequently asked questions' (FAQ) section of each airline's website and should also be clearly listed on your ticket or letter of confirmation. If in doubt, contact the airline directly and ask for written confirmation of your baggage allowance.

⬥ *Pretty painted house in Palaio Chorio, Alonnisos*

During your stay

AIRPORTS

Skiathos has the only international airport in the Sporades. The airport is 2 km (1 mile) east of Skiathos Town. Taxis and buses leave from immediately outside the arrivals hall and take around 5–10 minutes to town. Nowhere on the island is more than 30 minutes from the airport by car. Major car-rental companies with rental desks at the airport include Avis, Europcar, Hertz and Sixt.

The nearest airport on the mainland, at Volos, also receives charter flights from the UK from June to October and is 90–180 minutes from Skiathos, Skopelos and Alonnisos by frequent hydrofoil. Athens Eleftherios Venizelos International Airport is approximately 45 minutes from the city centre by public transport and is connected to central Athens by a new and efficient metro system. A taxi to central Athens takes around 35 minutes and taxis are available at all times.

COMMUNICATIONS

Local and international phone calls can be made from phone booths in the centre of most resorts and cities. These use only prepaid phonecards, which can be bought at post offices and most local shops. Mobile phone users subscribing to UK, Irish and mainland EU networks should experience no problems receiving or making calls anywhere in Greece; however, phones purchased in the USA, Canada, South Africa, Australia and New Zealand may not be able to access local networks.

There are Internet cafés, usually with broadband access, in the main villages of all three islands. All large hotels and many smaller hotels and guesthouses have Wi-Fi access for those travelling with a laptop; free Wi-Fi access is much more widely available in hotels now, or you can find an independent Internet café.

Post offices are marked by a prominent, circular yellow sign and can be found in most large villages. Stamps can be bought at post offices and in many gift shops and newsagents. Airmail letters take three to six days to reach EU countries; five to eight days to the USA and Canada;

TELEPHONING GREECE

The country code for Greece is 30. The prefixes for phoning Greece should be followed by the ten-digit local number.

From the UK, all EU countries and New Zealand: 00 30

From the USA and Canada: 011 30

From Australia: 0011 30

TELEPHONING FROM GREECE

These prefixes should be followed by the city code (minus the initial 0) and the subscriber's number.

To the UK: 00 44

To the USA or Canada: 001

To Ireland: 00 353

To Australia: 00 61

To New Zealand: 00 64

and slightly longer to Australia, New Zealand and South Africa. Postcards may take several weeks to reach their destination. Post offices are open 07.30–14.00 Monday to Friday.

CUSTOMS

Greeks are, by and large, talkative, hospitable and tolerant towards the ways of visitors. However, displays of public drunkenness and verbal aggression are generally unacceptable.

All Greek airports are regarded as security zones and photography, even of civil aircraft, is forbidden. You may also encounter signs forbidding photography in quite unexpected parts of the coast and at places such as reservoir dams and major road bridges. Never take photos or videos of any kind of military installation, or use binoculars anywhere near them, unless you want to risk a heavy fine or even several weeks or months in jail.

DRESS CODES

By almost any standard, Greece is a very easy-going country. Jacket and tie are not required even in the most expensive establishments, and most Greeks dress for comfort rather than formality, especially in summer. Topless sunbathing has become acceptable virtually everywhere. Total nudity is less acceptable except in secluded stretches of beach well away from main resort areas. However, shorts, sleeveless T-shirts and skimpy tops are unacceptable when visiting religious sites such as churches and monasteries, where the modesty code insists on long trousers and at least short-sleeved shirts for men and shirt or blouse and over-the-knee skirts or dresses for women. Some sites have modest attire for visitors to borrow, but don't rely on this.

ELECTRICITY

Voltage is 220 V. Sockets are standard EU, with two round pins. Visitors from the UK and North America will need adaptor plugs, which can be bought in many local shops. Most hotels and guesthouses can lend you an adaptor. Visitors from North America may need a step-down transformer for appliances using 110 V power supply.

EMERGENCIES

In the unlikely event of an emergency, dial the following numbers for emergency services:

Ambulance ☎ 166

Fire ☎ 199

General emergency (fire, police and medical) ☎ 100

For other health problems, try:

Skiathos Health Centre @ Skiathos Town ☎ 24270 22222

Skiathos GP surgery @ Skiathos Town ☎ 24270 29011

Skiathos dental surgery @ Skiathos Town ☎ 24270 21401/22384/ 23130/24300

Skiathos pharmacies @ Skiathos Town ☎ 24270 22988/21230/ 22666/24090

Skopelos Heath Centre ⊜ Skopelos Town ☎ 24240 22222
Skopelos GP surgery (private clinic) ⊜ Skopelos Town ☎ 24240 24555,
69999 24555
Alonnisos Health Centre ⊜ Patitiri ☎ 24240 65208

GETTING AROUND
Driving conditions
Roads on the islands are generally good and traffic is light except during
Greek holiday periods. However, island roads are very winding, with
many hairpin bends. Local driving habits can be erratic (as can be the
behaviour of visitors in rented cars or on scooters) and visiting drivers
should always use caution. Seat belts must be worn. Speed limits in
Greece are 50 kph (30 mph) in built-up areas, 80 kph (50 mph) outside
built-up areas, and 120 kph (74 mph) on motorways.

In the event of a breakdown, most car-rental agencies use the services
of one of the following:
ELPA (Automobile and Touring Club of Greece) ☎ 104
Express Service ☎ 154
Hellas Service ☎ 157

Car hire
Several international rental chains have desks at Skiathos airport. If you
only require a car for a day or two, local car-rental companies offer
adequately maintained vehicles at reasonable value for money, but if you
need a car for the whole of your stay it is usually cheaper to rent through
a major international company, an airline or your package tour operator
before leaving home. Full collision damage waiver (CDW), personal
accident insurance, bail bond and liability cover are essential. A full UK
or EU driving licence is valid but non-EU visitors need an international
driving licence.

Motorcycle & scooter rental
Motorcycles and scooters can be rented by the day or week from local
agencies at most resorts. Unless you are already a very experienced biker,

think twice before renting. Local roads, while well surfaced, are very winding, and local drivers show no mercy to two-wheelers. Many visitors are injured each year in motorcycle and scooter accidents. If you do rent a bike or scooter, wear a helmet at all times. Greek laws do not require bikers to wear helmets when riding within towns or villages, and you will see many locals riding without helmets. However, the risk of injury or death is just as high (if not higher) in built-up areas.

Motoring offences
Do not drink and drive. Penalties are severe and blood alcohol limits are set very low – one glass of wine or a half-litre of beer will take you over the limit. Police may impose on-the-spot fines for motoring offences.

Public transport
Buses and taxis Public transport on Skiathos is excellent, with buses every 15 minutes from 08.00 to 23.00 between Skiathos Town and Koukounaries, stopping approximately every 500 m (¼ mile) along the south coast. On Skiathos, water-taxis also loop around the island, picking up and dropping off at all the main resorts and beaches. On Skopelos and Alonnisos, public transport is minimal, and in practice the easiest way for the visitor to get around without using a rented car or scooter is by taxi.

Ferries Frequent high-speed hydrofoils and conventional ferries (up to six daily) connect Skiathos with Skopelos and Alonnisos and connect all three islands with the mainland ports of Agios Konstantinos and Volos and with Thessaloniki, Greece's second-largest city (about seven hours away). For up-to-date timetables, visit the Greek travel website Ⓦ www.gtp.gr, which also has links to online reservation sites. Tickets must be bought before boarding any hydrofoil or ferry – they cannot be bought on board.

HEALTH, SAFETY & CRIME
Eating and drinking in Greece is as safe as anywhere in Europe. Public-sector healthcare is generally acceptable. Private-sector clinics and

privately run hospitals operate to high standards and usually have English-speaking doctors and some English-speaking nursing staff.

Greece has no special health risks, but there are a number of minor nuisances that can spoil your holiday. Mosquitoes can be a pest in summer. Most guesthouse and hotel rooms come equipped with plug-in electric mosquito-repellent devices, but using a dab or two of repellent on exposed skin when going out after dark is advisable. On rocky parts of the beach, be careful not to tread on black sea urchins, whose spines can be very painful. In summer, Greek beaches can sometimes be plagued by larger numbers of jellyfish (*tsouchtres*), some of which can deliver an irritating but not dangerous sting.

Local insect life can sometimes be intimidating, but the large hornets and blue-black bees that often buzz around your veranda are harmless unless disturbed – leave them alone, and they will return the favour. Scorpions do exist, but are rarely seen and they too are harmless unless disturbed, with a painful but not lethal sting. Greeks detest all snakes, and will try to kill them on sight, but in fact Greece has no dangerous snakes, and most of its several species of snake are non-venomous.

Although there have been some protests and strikes against the government's fiscal austerity measures – occasionally violent – no visitor should expect to run into serious danger in Greece. Instances of violent crime against tourists are rare, but as in any holiday destination there is a risk of petty theft, so visitors should use normal caution on the beach and in bars and restaurants. Greece has been cited as the Mediterranean destination with the highest levels of alleged sexual assault against young British women. However, it is worth noting that many of the alleged assaults were by young British male visitors, not by Greek men.

Credit card fraud is an increasing problem in Greece. There are few precautions that you can take against your card being abused while in Greece, other than making sure that you are always present when it is being used. Be suspicious of shops or restaurants where waiters or shop assistants ask to take your card out of your sight for whatever reason –

always insist on being present while your card is being charged or authorised. Keep a personal record of all transactions, and scrutinise all charges closely for several months after you return. All major credit card companies offer insurance against credit card fraud and identity theft, and if you do not already have such a policy, consider taking one out before leaving home.

The police presence on all the islands is low (reflecting low crime levels). Most Greek police officers (who are armed and wear military-style navy-blue uniforms in summer) have a basic but not fluent grasp of English. At all costs avoid any situation that may become confrontational; Greek police tend to arrest first and ask questions later, and if you are arrested it may mean days or weeks in jail before your case comes before a magistrate.

An official 'tourist police' force exists, but is mainly involved with policing hotel and restaurant regulations. Port police – recognisable by their natty white uniforms and ubiquitous sunglasses – oversee all ferry operations at harbours and can usually provide up-to-the-minute information on ferry schedules.

MEDIA

Many bars in Skiathos resorts offer international satellite TV channels such as Sky Sports and Setanta. Some hotels also have in-room satellite TV, but the choice of English-language channels is usually limited to news channels such as BBC World and CNN. There are no local English-language newspapers, but most British daily and Sunday newspapers, including *The Times*, the *Daily Telegraph*, the *Daily Mail*, the *Daily Mirror* and the *Sun*, can be found at newsstands on Skiathos and Skopelos on the day after publication. The *International Herald Tribune* is also available on some newsstands and in large luxury hotels on the day of publication, and is co-published with an English-language translation of the major Greek national daily *Kathimerini*, so you can catch up on Greek local news as well as international events. If you have a portable short-wave radio, you can receive the BBC World Service on 9.41, 12.09 and 15.07 MHz.

OPENING HOURS

Opening hours on all the Sporades islands, as in all of Greece, are idiosyncratic. Despite government attempts to impose a nationwide regime of opening times for shops, bars, restaurants and other businesses, in practice most private enterprises open and close as they see fit.

Banks and post offices generally open from 08.00 until 14.00 Monday to Friday. Most small shops in resorts open around 09.00, close around 13.00–17.00, then reopen until at least 21.00. Restaurants usually open 12.00–15.00 for lunch, then reopen until around 23.00 for dinner. Some may stay open as late as 01.00, as do many cafés and music bars. In summer, some open-air dance clubs located well away from resort centres may stay open as late as 02.00. Markets usually open as early as 07.00 and close around 17.00 at the latest.

Opening hours for museums and archaeological sites under the aegis of the Greek Ministry of Culture are erratic, to say the least, and the hours actually in force often bear no relation to the officially published times. However, most museums and archaeological sites are open 08.30–15.00 Tues–Sun and are closed on Mondays.

RELIGION

For all practical purposes, to be Greek in the Sporades is to be Greek Orthodox, and it is extremely rare to meet anyone who professes any other religion.

TIME DIFFERENCES

Greek time is GMT +3 hours (Mar–Oct), GMT + 2 hours (Nov–Feb); US Eastern Standard Time +7 hours, US Pacific Standard Time +10 hours.

TIPPING

Tipping is not compulsory anywhere in Greece. Service is included in restaurants, and it is also normal practice to leave small change on the table when paying cash in bars and cafés – there is no fixed percentage. As anywhere else in the world, hotel porters welcome tips but there is no fixed rate. Taxi drivers do not expect to be tipped – although a gratuity for courteous and extra-helpful service is always appreciated.

TOILETS

Public toilets can be found in parks and squares, and at railway stations, bus terminals and airports. Standards are normally very high, and even public toilets in towns, villages, bus terminals and railway stations are generally kept much cleaner than in many other European countries, including Britain. Restaurant toilets are also usually clean but sometimes shabby. In almost all establishments, except for luxury hotels, you should drop used toilet paper in the bin provided, not in the lavatory bowl.

TRAVELLERS WITH DISABILITIES

People with disabilities will, in general, find it almost impossible to get around on Skiathos, Skopelos and Alonnisos, and it is also difficult in the Pilion on the mainland. Village streets are steep, cobbled and often potholed, there are numerous flights of steps to negotiate and there are no wheelchair ramps. Few smaller guesthouses and hotels, banks, restaurants or shops offer any kind of wheelchair access. Boarding buses, taxis and ferries is also very difficult for wheelchair users.

Holiday Care (📞 0845 124 9971 🌐 www.holidaycare.org.uk) provides information for people with disabilities travelling from the UK.

Disability Now is a Greek non-profit organisation. Its website contains some information in English and its volunteers may also be able to answer (in English, via email) specific questions about travel in Greece for people with disabilities. 🌐 www.disabled.gr
📧 info@disabled.gr

ACKNOWLEDGEMENTS

The publishers would like to thank the following for providing their copyright photographs for this book: Alamy page 37; BigStockPhoto page 72; Chris Deliso pages 61, 97; Dreamstime (Violetta Dounia) page 53; Terry Harris pages 42, 77, 84; Thomas Cook Publishing page 49; www.sargasso-travelimages.com pages 5, 9, 10–11, 13, 19, 21, 24, 29, 31, 35, 40, 47, 50, 57, 58, 62, 64, 67, 71, 78, 81, 88, 91, 93, 101, 103, 105, 109, 115.

Project editor: Penny Isaac
Layout: Donna Pedley
Proofreaders: Caroline Hunt & Kelly Walker
Indexer: Karolin Thomas

Send your thoughts to
books@thomascook.com

- Found a beach bar, peaceful stretch of sand or must-see sight that we don't feature?

- Like to tip us off about any information that needs a little updating?

- Want to tell us what you love about this handy little guidebook and, more importantly, how we can make it even handier?

Then here's your chance to tell all! Send us ideas, discoveries and recommendations today and then look out for your valuable input in the next edition of this title.

Email to the above address or write to:
pocket guides Series Editor, Thomas Cook Publishing, PO Box 227, Unit 9, Coningsby Road, Peterborough PE3 8SB, UK

Useful phrases

English	Greek	Approx pronunciation

BASICS

English	Greek	Approx pronunciation
Yes	Ναι	*Ne*
No	Οχι	*O-khee*
Please	Παρακαλώ	*Pa-ra-ka-lh*
Thank you	Ευχαριστώ	*Ef-ha-ri-**sto***
Hello	Γεια σας	*Ya sas*
Goodbye	Αντίο	*An**dee**o*
Excuse me	Με συγχωρείτε	*Me si-nho-**ri**-te*
Sorry	Συγγνώμη	*Sig-**no**-mi*
That's okay	Εντάξει	*En-**ta**-xi*
I don't speak Greek	Δεν μιλώ Ελληνικά	*Den Mi-**lo** (E-li-ni-**ka**)*
Do you speak English?	Μιλάτε Αγγλικά;	*Mi-**la**-te an-gli-**ka**?*
Good morning	Καλημέρα	*Ka-li-**me**-ra*
Good afternoon	χαίρετε	***He**-re-te*
Good evening	Καλησπέρα	*Ka-li-**spe**-ra*
Goodnight	Καληνύχτα	*Ka-li-**nih**-ta*
My name is ...	Ονομάζομαι	*O-no-**ma**-zo-me*

NUMBERS

English	Greek	Approx pronunciation
One	Ένα	***E**-na*
Two	Δύο	***Di**-o*
Three	Τρία	***Tri**-a*
Four	Τέσσερα	***Te**-se-ra*
Five	Πέντε	***Pen**-te*
Six	Έξι	***E**-xi*
Seven	Επτά	*Ep-**ta***
Eight	Οκτώ	*Ok-**to***
Nine	Εννέα	***E**-ne-a*
Ten	Δέκα	***De**-ka*
Twenty	Είκοσι	***I**-ko-si*
Fifty	Πενήντα	*Pe-**nin**-ta*
One hundred	Εκατό	*E-ka-**to***

SIGNS & NOTICES

English	Greek	Approx pronunciation
Airport	Αεροδρόμιο	*A-e-rodromio*
Railway station	Σιδηροδρομικός εταμς	*Sidirodromikos Stathmos*
Smoking/ non-smoking	Για Καπνιστές/ Για μη καπνιστές	*Ya kapnistes/ Ya mikapnistes*
Toilets	Τουαλέτα	*Tualeta*
Ladies/Gentlemen	Γυναικών/Ανδρών	*Yinekon/Andron*